Best Hikes With
CHILDREN™
in Colorado

Best Hikes With
CHILDREN™
in Colorado

Maureen Keilty
Photos by Dan Peha

The Mountaineers

4 3 2
5 4 3 2

Published by The Mountaineers
1011 S.W. Klickitat Way, Suite 107, Seattle, Washington 98134

Published simultaneously in Canada by Douglas & McIntyre, Ltd., 1615 Venables Street, Vancouver, B.C. V5L 2H1

Published simultaneously in Great Britain by Cordee, 3a DeMontfort Street, Leicester, England, LE1 7HD

Manufactured in the United States of America

Edited by Lorretta Palagi
Maps by Dan Peha
All photographs by Dan Peha
Cover design by Betty Watson
Book design by Bridget Culligan
Frontispiece: A flower-dappled aspen glen near Crested Butte

Library of Congress Cataloging in Publication Data

Keilty, Maureen, 1952–
   Best hikes with children in Colorado / Maureen Keilty.
      p. cm.
   Includes index.
   ISBN 0-89886-280-9
   1. Hiking—Colorado—Guide-books. 2. Family recreation—Colorado—Guide-books. 3. Colorado—Description and travel—1981– —Guide-books.   I. Title.
GV199.42.C6K45   1991
917.88′0433—dc20   91-6702
                                                                CIP

To Niko, for child-testing every hike in this book

Teach your children what we have taught our children—that the earth is our mother. Whatever befalls the earth, befalls the sons of the earth. If men spit upon the ground, they spit themselves.

This we know. The earth does not belong to man; man belongs to the earth. This we know. All things are connected like the blood that unites one family. All things are connected...

Chief Seattle

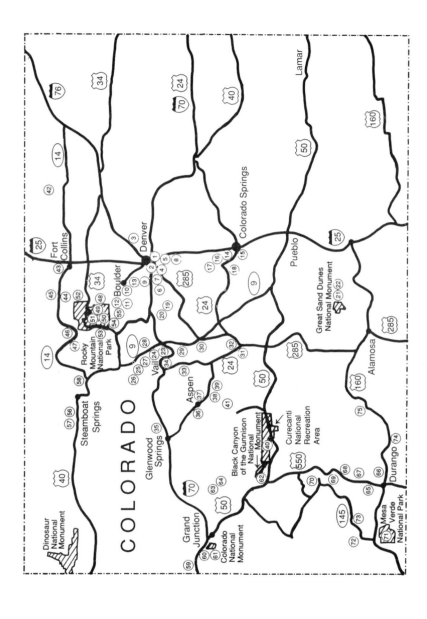

Contents

Legend

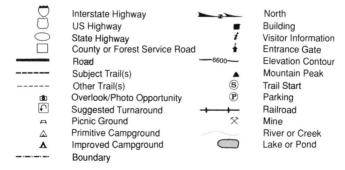

Interstate Highway		North	
US Highway		Building	
State Highway		*i* Visitor Information	
County or Forest Service Road		Entrance Gate	
Road		—6600— Elevation Contour	
Subject Trail(s)		▲ Mountain Peak	
Other Trail(s)		Ⓢ Trail Start	
Overlook/Photo Opportunity		Ⓟ Parking	
Suggested Turnaround		Railroad	
Picnic Ground		✕ Mine	
Primitive Campground		River or Creek	
Improved Campground		Lake or Pond	
Boundary			

Acknowledgments

I wish to thank the employees of the U.S. Forest Service, National Park Service, and the divisons of parks and recreation in numerous cities along the Front Range for providing me with both verbal and written trail information. I thank Stuart McDonald, Colorado State Trail Coordinator, for his assistance in selecting appropriate trails. Many friends' tips on trails are likewise appreciated. Thanks go to John Zwisler of Xerographics Plus and to Sarah Taylor of Customized Personnel, both of Durango, for providing copy service when I needed it most.

The late Craig Colvig is credited for giving me my start in hiking and the impetus to keep going on almost any kind of trail. Gary and Jane Ferguson are recognized for providing the inspiration to write about the natural world. Finally, special thanks go to my husband Dan Peha, for adding an adventuresome spirit to all our hikes, and later, checking for accuracy in each of my trail descriptions.

Introduction

If there is but one inexpensive and enjoyable route to family fun, hiking the trails in Colorado's national forests and parks is it. From the four-year-old hiker marveling at the "sparkly" rock she found along the trail, to the dad interpreting a topographical map to his son, hiking rewards all members of the family.
Keeping the hikes fun for everyone in the family requires some preparation.

Keeping it Fun

Setting the Scene

Enthusiastically introducing a hike sparks eagerness in your children. They'll sense your confidence and desire to discover nature and will want to join the outdoor venture.

Describe the hike with words such as "explore," "walk," or "along the way, we'll see... " Try not to use words such as "hard," "easy," or "difficult." Tell your children about the destination and, more importantly, that they will be able to stop to look at animal tracks, smell flowers, or maybe listen for the bugle call of an elk. Exploring the sights, sounds, textures, aromas, and even flavors along the trail can be as rewarding as the destination itself.

Spontaneity

Spontaneity can redirect your trip or simply season it with a variety of interests. The natural curiosity of children can lead to examining insects under a rock or discovering a flower that smells like peanut butter. While walking through a spruce forest once with a small group of young girls, I heard the hoo-ooo of an owl. Looking into the dark canopy overhead, my eyes caught movement of a large bird fluttering its wings. I gathered the girls

Kids cuddle in a boulder pile near Mount Evans.

away from the tree where for nearly two hours we watched a downy young barn owl take its first flights while its mother observed from a distant branch. We never made it to the hot spring as planned, but were warmed by the gift we shared.

No doubt your child will discover something you simply know nothing about. When your son asks the name of a snail captured in his palm and you have to respond with "I don't know," enhance his discovery anyway by asking "How does it see? Can you find its mouth? Do you suppose it can hear us talk? . . . "

Hike Leaders

Assign a hike leader. Somehow this revered status gives kids an energy boost and encourages them to pay closer attention to the map and watch for landmarks. Switching the title to a child whose energy is waning keeps the group moving at a steady pace. It's a good idea to let your young leaders know in advance where this "change of command" is to take place.

Complaints, aches, and pains will be lessened considerably if your child brings a companion along. Neither will want to appear slow in front of the other and the two will concoct unheard-of games.

Patience, Praise, and Playfulness

Frequent fuel stops as in "We'll have a drink of water and some gorp when we reach the top of this hill" also keep the hike moving. But keep the rest stops brief. Breath-catching stops during high-altitude climbs should be thirty seconds to a minute and a half. Breaks in hiking that last longer than five minutes can defeat the purpose of stopping. Not only do they increase the hiking time considerably, but they cause children, and adults, to loose their motivation. This is because the drive to get going again diminishes as the cardiovascular system slows down. You have to start all over to attain the efficiency your climbing muscles had prior to stopping. A group that stands during its rest stops will want to keep moving.

As most parents know, praise and patience are two ingredients on which children thrive. On a hike, be liberal with both. Plan the trip so there's time to play a balancing game while crossing the creek or to watch a beaver reappear from its den. Compliments given early in the trip are more effective than those used later to encourage tired hikers. Your interest in your children's discoveries will fuel their energy. Let your children know how proud you are of their hiking strength and that they picked up trash along the trail. Praise given in the presence of other children and adults has a lasting influence.

When children lose interest during a hike, turn the trip into a fun stroll. Try skipping or walking backward. Walk in bare feet. (Be sure the trail surface is free of sharp objects.) Sing a song the kids know and can join in on. Encourage the hike leader to make up his or her own way of walking that the others should copy. Or, try any of the following techniques, which are sure to eliminate tedium from most any trek:

Silent fox walk. Instruct children to place each step with their weight coming down on the outside of the foot and rolling to the inside. With practice they'll move with fluidity and silence.

Color match. While walking, children should look for colors in nature to match the colors of the clothing they are wearing.

Open house. Insect and animal homes abound in the forest. Have children watch for bird nests, spider webs, insect galls (growth-like swellings holding insect eggs, which are attached to twigs in a bush or leaf stems), a ground squirrel's entrance hole, a creek, rotten logs, and other examples of woodland creatures' homes.

Sniff a tree. Hug a tree and discover its aroma; the ponderosa pine has a delightful vanilla-like scent.

Bird music. Listen for bird calls and try to mimic their melodies and rhythms.

Fantasy fun. Mark Twain once said, "You can't depend on your eyes when your imagination is out of focus." During a long hike, you can lift tired spirits by skipping along the trail, pretending it's the "yellow brick road." Salute the rocks guarding the mountain. Compliment the creek for its song. Introduce yourself to the Engelmann spruce. Shake hands with its branches. Sing to the mushroom. Keep your imagination in focus—it can be contagious.

What in the woods. In your mind, select a natural item your group sees frequently while hiking. Your children guess the item by asking questions that require a "yes" or "no" response. The child who names it selects the next item to be "what in the woods."

Feeding free. Living creatures depend on each other for their food. A squirrel scampering through the woods with a pinecone in its mouth, a red-winged blackbird alighting on a cattail, and a mushroom erupting from a rotting log are examples of one species feeding the other. Show your children some examples and ask them to point out others as they walk.

Finding feelers. "Touch something smooth." "Feel a fuzzy thing." "Find something slippery." Hands-on touching energizes tired minds and feet.

When It Rains

Sudden weather changes are the norm for Colorado's mountains. During the summer months, rain showers can be expected midafternoon in the high country, so it's best to start your hike early in the day. Regardless of when you start the hike or how clear the sky looks, rain gear, including a waterproof hood or hat, is a must for every hiker.

The safest place to be during a rainstorm is in a thick stand of trees. If, while following a trail above the timberline, you notice clouds building, head down to tree level *pronto*. The severity of rain and your children's ages will determine whether your group gathers under cover of shrubs or continues walking back to the trailhead. Whatever choice is made, your positive attitude will keep fears at bay.

Time spent waiting out a rainstorm, whether you are huddled below a shrub or under the roofed section of an abandoned cabin, can be fun for youngsters. A magnifying glass, tucked away in your backpack for just such occasions, will occupy fidgety children. Or a string laid across the forest floor for them to walk their fingers along along gives them an opportunity to pretend they are ants walking a nature trail.

That leftover apple from lunch can be put to good use while you are waiting for the storm to subside. Before showing it to your listeners, tell them a colorful version of this story: One day a little boy had nothing to do, so he asked his mother for a game. The mother told him to go outside and find a "little red house without windows or doors and a star inside." Be descriptive about the places in the forest where the boy searched. Include the plants and animals he spoke to, asking where he might find the little red house with no windows or doors and a star inside. When the boy returned home he stopped in an orchard and asked the wind to help him find the little red house. Just then, the wind shook an apple from the tree. The boy realized it was little, red, and it had no windows or doors. (Present your apple.) To find the star inside, he cut the apple in half (be sure to cut it horizontally) and sure enough—there was a star! (formed by the seed/core arrangement). Children enjoy eating segments of the little red house as much as they like listening to the story.

Of Mountains, Mesas, and Forests

It's your choice—a gentle saunter along a babbling creek deep in a forest, a rigorous trek across the flower-dappled tundra, or a sandy walk past ancient ruins and thorny cacti. Hikes in Colorado cross the biological, geological, even historical spectrum. Having even a tad of understanding about these worlds makes each hike all the more memorable.

A staircase is perhaps the simplest way to describe the arrangement of Colorado's plant and animal life zones. Beginning at Colorado's eastern border, the bottom step at 3500 feet to 5500 feet is the Upper Sonoran life zone. Characterized by grass-blanketed prairies, sandy bluffs, and a few marsh areas, this relatively dry life zone is canyon sculpted in many places. In its forests grow drought-resistant pinyon and juniper trees with a wide variety of grasses, cacti, and yucca adding soft greens and yellows to the landscape. Birds of prey feed and nest in the canyons of this region, and bands of pronghorn antelope race across its plains. For a sampling of this life zone, see the Pawnee Buttes Trail, hike 42.

The next step to the west, at 5500 to 8000 feet, is called the Foothills, or Transition, zone. As its second name implies, plants and animals from the plains and the higher altitude coniferous forests converge here. Ponderosa pine trees dominate its south-facing slopes, while Douglas firs take hold on the hilltops. Blue spruce, cottonwoods, and willows can be found along its streams. Many of the hikes taking place in and around the Denver, Boulder, and Colorado Springs areas can be considered Foothills hikes.

The Transition zone, at 7500 feet, covers a large portion of Western Colorado. Although it is considered sagebrush country, which is generally dry and sun-exposed, fingers of lush streambeds and dense forests are woven into this region. A classic example of this diverse terrain can be found on the Waldo Canyon Loop, hike 16.

One step up and to the west of the Front Range is the Boreal region, which includes the state's mountains. With a range of 8000 to 14,000 feet, this zone is divided into three sections: the Canadian at 8000 to 11,000 feet, the Hudsonian or timberline at 11,000 to 11,500 feet, and the Alpine zone, which includes the frosty, wind-swept terrain above the timberline.

Wildflowers and aspens proliferate in the Canadian zone, which is also home to several varieties of spruce and pine tree. A large percentage of the hikes in this book take place here, considered by many the prettiest of Colorado's many ecosystems.

The narrowest of life zone, the Hudsonian, displays stands of beautifully wind-sculpted bristlecone pine trees. Engelmann spruce and subalpine fir are also shaped by the strong winds and heavy snow of the region. A good example of this timberline world is the Mount Goliath Trail, hike 19.

The Alpine zone, which begins where the trees end, consists of pockets of tiny wildflowers tucked into a harsh, treeless tundra. Most hikers come this far to feast their eyes on the mountaintops' magnificent vistas, only to discover that equally precious sights are at their feet. Several ecosystems exist in this land above the trees, which can be discovered on the Ute Trail Tundra Walk, hike 51.

What to Take

Boots

Starting from the feet up, hiking boots, properly fitted and broken in, are a prerequisite for enjoyable hiking. Sneakers or running shoes work well for the short, paved trails in this book, and may be adequate for longer treks where the trail is relatively free of rock and tree roots. However, boots are a necessity for full dayhikes and backpack trips. For children, wearing them somehow gives the hike a special importance.

Unfortunately, hiking boots for youngsters are expensive—especially since some children outgrow them in one season. Other than boots found at used clothing stores or at yard sales, the least costly hiking shoes are simply high-top sneakers. Those made of leather or a similar stiff material provide the needed ankle sup-

A proud angler at Mesa Lake

port. Lugged soles help grip slippery rock surfaces and provide traction on muddy terrain.

For those buying hiking boots, timing is the first consideration. Plan to shop well in advance of a hiking trip. Time spent wearing hiking boots around the house or around the block is a necessity for breaking them in before the hike. When they are trying on the boots, children should wear heavy socks. Make sure the boot is snug enough to prevent rubbing, but not so tight it pinches the toes. Boots improperly fitted or not broken in can ruin the most spectacular summit climb. I still remember, at the top of the first 14,000-foot peak I climbed, the miserable, teary-eyed face of a young hiker in our group whose new boots she said were "torture chambers." Children forced to hike under such conditions won't relish doing it again, regardless of your enthusiasm.

Packs

Another hiking requirement, at least for children, is a pack. Even beginning walkers like shouldering at least some of the "essentials" (see next section) as well as their "very own" raincoat or water bottle. For longer treks, those that involve an overnight camp, larger daypacks or backpacks are needed. Make the packing process a group project, giving each hiker an opportunity to select what he or she carries. Take time to show children how to load the pack evenly and how to attach the sleeping bag or tent fly securely. Tell children that it's important they remember what they carry in their packs. This prevents the repeated "Who's got the gorp?" and "Where's the map?" questions that whittle away rest stops. Use this time to fit the pack properly by adjusting its straps. Remind children that once the pack is loaded they are not to sit on it unless, of course, they like eating squashed apples and cracker crumbs for lunch.

Let each child know that he or she is carrying something the entire group needs. Whether it's a bag of quick-energy chocolates or the map and first-aid kit, if the young hiker believes the items in his or her pack are important, the child will feel like an important member of the group.

The Ten Essentials

The Mountaineers, over years of teaching mountaineering, have developed a list of ten items that should be carried on every hike. The "Ten Essentials" provide comfort and the necessities for coping with emergencies caused by foul weather, an injury, or other unexpected incidents.

1. **Extra clothing.** Another layer of warm clothing is a hedge against wet or torn pants or sudden weather changes. Include a knit hat in the pack.
2. **Extra food.** An extra high-energy bar per person (preferably hidden in your pack) is a reliable measure against hungry, irritable hikers should the trip take longer than planned.

3. **Sunglasses.** Bright, high-altitude sunshine can tire little eyes. Too much sun exposure can also damage the eyes.
4. **Firestarter candle or chemical fuel.** During an unforeseen overnight camp, the campfire will be a lifesaver.
5. **Matches in a waterproof container.** A fire is not possible without reliable matches, which are available at sporting goods stores.
6. **Pocketknife.** One of the most useful items.
7. **First-aid kit.** Check to make sure it's complete and hope it's not needed.
8. **Flashlight.** Keep fresh batteries in it and hope it's not needed to guide children down a trail at night.
9. **Map.** Always carry a map of the overall area you are hiking in.
10. **Compass.** Orient yourself with the compass and the map before setting foot on the trail.

To make the getting ready process quicker, keep as many of these essentials as possible gathered together in one location. Children require additional items as described below.

Sunscreen is essential in Colorado for even the most seasoned hikers. Even overcast days cay result in serious skin burns for unprotected skin. Select a sunscreen lotion that is formulated for children and test it before leaving home. A lip balm with sun protection could be carried in most every hiker's pocket.

Insect repellent, for example the tiny one-ounce squeeze bottle type, is worth several hundred pounds of protection. No-see-ums, common in sagebrush country, prowl invisibly around the ear. Protect the ear from their irritating welts by dabbing a few drops of the repellent around the neck area.

A whistle, carried by each child who understands that it should be used only in an emergency, can aid in locating a lost little one.

Pack your first-aid kit with additional medicine or supplies your child needs. Extra toilet paper and plastic bags to carry it in are also suggested. A change of underwear and socks can erase the memory of an embarrassing accident and allow the trip to continue.

A shovel or trowel for personal sanitation use is also recommended. A pair of pliers and an extra rain tarp are useful items. If soap is necessary, bring only a biodegradable variety. Be aware,

A family studies the map before setting out.

however, that all soap pollutes lakes and streams.

String or a shoelace can be of practical use as well as a trail marker used in, for example, pretending to be ants walking a nature trail, mentioned earlier. A bandanna, magnifying lens, paper and pencil, a small paper bag, even a tiny book of stories are useful tools for examining the environment or passing time during a summer storm.

Trail Treats

For some little hikers, special trail food is the biggest attraction to the sport. Children like selecting the nuts and dried fruit for the gorp and can be helpful in preparing other items like carrot sticks, little containers of peanut butter, or packages of crackers. Encourage children to suggest their favorite finger food and, for overnight trips, a one-pot meal such as macaroni and cheese, tuna and noodles, chili, etc.

For the most part, freeze-dried dinners, despite their gourmet-sounding names, do not fare well with children. Stay with their favorites or try new concoctions of grains and dehydrated vegetables at home before introducing them to hungry hikers on the trail. Health food stores carry a wide variety of grains and dehydrated foods such as fruit, vegetables, cheese, and tomato powder. Ask a clerk at the store for recommended trail food items.

After the food is packaged and divided up, show children how and where to pack their allotment in an accessible, somewhat crush-proof location.

Backcountry Safety

Just as walking to school entails a certain amount of risk, so does hiking any of the trails described in this book. Safety is not a measure of how easy or challenging the trail is rated. It's a product of common sense coupled with preparation and a positive attitude.

Every effort has been made to describe these trails as accurately as possible. Weather and trail use, however, can alter the trail condition from day to day. Trail maintenance, or lack thereof, can also influence the trip considerably. Your physical condition has as much bearing on the hike as does the weather or the route. If a youngster is showing signs that the hike is doing more harm than good, be prepared to turn around. Before leaving, make the child feel a destination has been reached and that the trip was a success.

Drinking Water

No matter how pure the mountain stream or lake appears, the water in it should be considered unsafe for drinking until properly treated.

The most common threat to backcountry water sources is the presence of *Giardia* cysts, which are microscopic and transmitted primarily by animals (and some humans). Flu-like symptoms of giardiasis—from stomach cramps to severe diarrhea—appear in five to fourteen days and can last as long as six weeks if untreated. Taking prescription medication is the only cure for this potentially serious disease.

Do not drink or brush teeth with any water that is untreated. Dayhikers should be able to carry all the liquids they require. But if you are backpacking, use a water filter or a chemical treatment system. Otherwise, water should be boiled at least ten minutes before drinking.

It's better to start each trek with a day's supply of drinking water for each person. One quart per person is sufficient for most dayhikes less than four hours long. Thirst isn't always an indicator of water need. Dehydration, its first symptom often being a headache, results when adults drink less than two quarts of water per day. Up to four quarts is needed for strenuous, high-altitude activities. Another sign of too little water is dark yellow urine. Remember, stamina is diminished as much as 25 percent when an adult loses one and one-half quarts of water.

Hypothermia

Hypothermia, the lowering of internal body temperature, is a serious threat to hikers exposed to cool temperatures. Wind, exhaustion, and wetness aggravate this number one killer of outdoor recreationists. Most cases develop in air temperatures of 30 to 50 degrees.

Due to their relatively small body sizes, children show signs of hypothermia sooner than adults exposed to the same conditions. Whiny, uncooperative, or listless children are exhibiting the first signs of hypothermia. More advanced symptoms include uncontrollable fits of shivering, slurred speech, frequent stumbling, memory lapses, and apparent exhaustion even after a rest. Many hypothermia victims, children particularly, deny feeling cold, so watch for the other signs.

Staying dry is probably the best way to prevent hypothermia. Wet clothing loses about 90 percent of its insulating value. Wool loses less heat than cotton and some synthetic fabrics. Prevent getting wet when the rain starts—it's next to impossible to get dry during a rainstorm. Early morning and late afternoon and evening are times when children are generally tired. Pay close attention to your child's conditions at these times, especially during cool, overcast days.

Treatment for hypothermia begins with getting the victim out of the rain and wind. Remove all wet clothes and replace them with warm, dry ones. A warm sleeping bag may be needed and skin-to-skin contact is necessary for serious hypothermia cases.

Altitude Sickness

Severe headaches, nausea, a cough, lack of appetite, or a staggering gait are indications that a person is not acclimatized to high altitudes. Lowlanders, children in particular, should spend at least two to three days acclimatizing to Colorado's high altitudes. For hikes beginning at elevations of more than 9000 feet, plan to ascend no more than 1000 feet per day.

Encourage children with signs of altitude sickness to breathe deeply, rest, and eat high-energy foods. Aspirin can alleviate headaches. If symptoms persist, head for lower elevations.

Staying Found

Ardent butterfly chasers are apt to lose their way. All children, be they adventuresome or stay-on-the-trail types, should

Poison ivy—DON'T TOUCH!!

know what to do should they discover they have been separated from the group. Tell them to stay in one place. Don't go in search of the trail or other people. Encourage them to use the whistle; three blasts is an international distress call. Wait—help is on the way. Tell children they will be found sooner if they sit in an open area.

Prevent lost hikers by assigning every hiker a partner. Remind children they are to stay on the trail at all times. When the trail meets another one, children who have gone ahead must wait for the rest of the group. Let the hike leader know he or she should stop the hike at various intervals to make certain everyone is keeping up. At camp, show children the boundaries within which they can explore on their own. Walk to the water pump and toilet with children so they know the path.

Environmental Etiquette

Hiking in Colorado's forests and mountains brings a great sense of freedom, but with that comes the responsibility to leave the land in its wild state. The following reminders are in no way all-inclusive.

Stay on the Trail

Walking alongside the trail tramples vegetation and widens it. Do not allow youngsters to cut across switchbacks to go downhill faster—water will follow their new path and soon damage the trail.

Pack It Out

Trash of any kind must be packed out. After a fuel stop, check for discarded nutshells, orange peels, or cellophane wrappings. A potato chip, though it may decompose, can also cause a serious digestive upset for unlucky chipmunks.

How and Where "To Go"

Remind children to use toilet facilities before the start of the hike. While on the trail, teach your children to urinate at least 200 feet from a water source or campsite. It is no longer acceptable to bury toilet paper; animals dig it up. Carry it out in a plastic bag. Human waste should be deposited at least 200 feet from a water source, in a hole six inches deep, capped by the sod or soil taken from the same spot.

Don't Pick the Flowers

Little hands are prone to pick bouquets of wildflowers. To prevent this innocent elimination of trailside beauty, I explain to young hikers that wildflowers are like you and me; they cannot live if their bottom half, the stems, are broken off or put in a glass of water. I tell the children it makes me sad to see flowers taken from their home. (It's illegal to pick Colorado's state flower, the columbine, in any of the state's parks.) When your child finds other alluring items such as "sparkly" rocks or deer antlers, say: "I wonder if the next hiker will have eyes as sharp as yours and see this pretty... "

Walk and Speak Softly

These trails take you into the homes of deer and elk, marmots and pikas, eagles, hawks, and hummingbirds, even bears, mountain lions, and foxes. Noise destroys the tranquillity needed to sight forest creatures. Speaking in a quiet tone will remind your children that they are visiting a home where peace is needed. Perhaps the sighting of a coyote or family of ermine will reward their hushed behavior.

Selecting a Campsite

Camping in these forests requires minimum impact practices. To avoid harming plant life, choose a campsite well away from the trail in an established site or on a non-vegetated patch. Use a gas stove for cooking. If your young hikers want a campfire, keep it small and in a pit, preferably in an established campfire site. Use only fallen dead wood; don't break limbs off trees. Drown the fire with water. (A good way to make sure the fire is out is to check it by running your fingers through the soaked ashes.) Scatter the ashes and leftover wood. If you created the firepit, fill the depression with the soil and sod originally taken from it. Dish washing should take place away from the water source. The best pot scrubber I know of is a smidgen of wet sand or gravel applied with a bit of elbow grease. If soap is used, be sure it's biodegradable. Leftover food should be packed out.

Careless campers leave a "hurtful sight," as one young hiker told me. Your group will feel better if they contribute to cleaning up the natural environment. I've seen many children at the end of a hike proudly empty their pockets of gum wrappers and cigarette butts found along the trail. Report any serious violation to the

Creating a sand castle along the Roaring Fork River

trail at the nearest forest ranger office.

Above all, enjoy the grand vistas of the mountains as well as the intimate panoramas at your feet.

How to Use This Book

The hikes described in this guidebook represent the best of Colorado's diverse ecosystems. All the trails selected are near or en route to popular destinations in the state. Thus, most of the hikes don't require driving far into remote regions, and all are two-wheel-drive accessible. The book is arranged into four zones with seventeen to twenty-two hikes in each.

The Metro zone includes trails in and around the Denver, Boulder, Colorado Springs, and Mount Evans areas. Two hikes from the Great Sand Dunes National Monument are listed in this section.

The Central zone lists trails in areas around Summit County, Vail, Aspen, Crested Butte, and the Black Canyon of Gunnison National Monument.

Fort Collins, Rocky Mountain National Park, and Steamboat Springs are the access points for the hikes in the Northern zone.

Southwestern and Western Colorado trails are represented in the West/Southwest zone. Starting destinations include Grand Junction, Durango, and Mesa Verde.

Each hike description begins with an information block summarizing important information on distance, elevation gain, maps, etc. Driving directions to the trailhead are included in the next paragraph. The hike directions and narration are bordered by one of several symbols (see p. 32 for a key to these symbols). Turnaround points indicate a fine spot to enjoy the view and turn around with a feeling of having completed the hike. A caution symbol indicates perilous cliffs, tricky crossings, or steep terrain. Specific environmental elements along the trail are also indicated with a symbol and provide a learning tool for parents and hike leaders. Each of these environmental close-ups is designed to involve children in learning from and respecting nature.

Hikes are rated easy, moderate, and challenging. Rather than define the criteria for what makes a hike easy, moderate, or challenging, I relied on a variety of factors. Elevation gain, trail condition, and distance were important when figuring this label. Equally important were what the hikers I met on the trail had to say about it. Also, because I was seven, eight, or nine months pregnant while hiking each of these trails, my evaluations reflected a child's endurance. Each hike, I can safely say, has been child-tested!

The "hikable" listing in the information block refers to the approximate months the trail is snow-free or open to the public. Winter snowfall and spring temperatures can alter these dates considerably. It's a good idea to call the nearest ranger station for

A bird's-eye view of the San Juan Mountains

an update on the trail's condition before attempting the hike early or late in the season.

All of these hikes can be completed during the day and range in length from 0.3 to 5.5 miles one way. Whenever possible, loop trips were selected. On these, the trail takes a circuitous route back to the trailhead. Turnaround spots marked in the trail description indicate ideal destinations for a short hike and/or a picnic lunch stop. Many of the hikes can be extended into overnight or backpack trips.

Hikers interested in learning more about using maps in the wilderness should refer to USGS maps. Not every trail in the

Fun wheeling in the clouds

state is marked on these maps; however, the trails in this book with a USGS listing are listed as such and can be found on the map named in the information block. It's a good idea to acquaint yourself with USGS topographical maps by orienting yourself with a compass while on a well-marked, perhaps familiar, trail and land area.

Wheelchair accessibility simply reflects that portions of the trail are level enough for limited wheelchair use. Having spent enough time in a wheelchair to know I missed hiking, I now watch for barrier-free trails. At the time of this writing, Forest Service districts throughout the state were proposing numerous wheelchair-accessible trails. For a listing of many of Colorado's wheelchair-accessible trails, see the Appendix. Before leaving, it's advisable to call the number listed with each trail to learn its condition.

A Note About Safety

Safety is an important concern in all outdoor activities. No guidebook can alert you to every hazard or anticipate the limitations of every reader. Therefore, the descriptions of roads, trails, routes, and natural features in this book are not representations that a particular place or excursion will be safe for your party. When you follow any of the routes described in this book, you assume responsibility for your own safety. Under normal conditions, such excursions require the usual attention to traffic, road and trail conditions, weather, terrain, the capabilities of your party, and other factors. Keeping informed on current conditions and exercising common sense are the keys to a safe, enjoyable outing.

The Mountaineers

Key to Symbols

 Dayhikes. These are hikes that can be completed in a single day. While some trips allow camping, only a few require it.

 Backpack trips. These are hikes whose length or difficulty makes camping out either necessary or recommended for most families.

 Easy trails. These are relatively short, smooth, gentle trails suitable for small children or first-time hikers.

 Moderate trails. Most of these are 2 to 4 miles total distance and feature more than 500 feet of elevation gain. The trail may be rough and uneven. Hikers should wear lug-soled boots and be sure to carry the Ten Essentials.

 Difficult trails. These are often rough, with considerable elevation gain or distance to travel. They are suitable for older or experienced children. Lug-soled boots and the Ten Essentials are standard equipment.

 Hikable. The best times of year to hike each trail are indicated by the following symbols: flower—spring; sun—summer; leaf—fall; snowflake—winter.

 Driving directions. These paragraphs tell you how to get to the trailheads.

 Turnarounds. These are places, mostly along moderate trails, where families can cut their hike short yet still have a satisfying outing. Turnarounds usually offer picnic opportunities, views, or special natural attractions.

 Cautions. These mark potential hazards—cliffs, stream or highway crossing, and the like—where close supervision of children is strongly recommended.

 Environmental close-ups. These highlight special environmental elements along the trail and help children learn about and respect nature.

METRO

(Denver, Colorado Springs, Boulder)

1. High Line Canal Trail

Location: Denver Metro Area
Type: Dayhike
Difficulty: Easy for children
Hikable: Year-round
Distance: Variable
Starting elevation: 5280 feet
High point: 5280 feet
Map: Denver Metro Trails Guide
Wheelchair accessible

Driving Directions: The High Line Canal can be reached from many streets as shown on the map given here. You may also obtain a Denver Metro Trails Guide map by sending a self-addressed stamped (postage for 2 ounces) envelope to the Division of Parks, 1313 Sherman Street, Denver, CO 80203. Each section offers a calm reprieve from the city and a chance to savor a slice of the environment.

For a refreshing pause amid Denver's bustle, enjoy a quiet walk along the High Line Canal. Conceived in 1870 by James Duff, a Scotsman determined to bring water to the farms east of

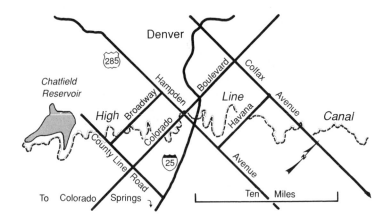

Ducks are frequent visitors to the ponds near the High Line Canal.

Denver, the 71-mile waterway is still an irrigation canal, but for Denverites it is better known as a swath of nature that runs through the heart of a city.

The 58-mile-long, 12-foot-wide pathway (paved in urban areas, hard-packed south of Hampden Avenue) parallels the canal, which carries water 4 to 7 feet deep. Beginning in South Platte Canyon (south Denver), the canal follows the natural contours of the land, dropping only 300 feet in elevation for its entire length. The trail's southeast to northwest course traverses open plains and urban sections, and passes near beautiful residential areas, parks, and golf courses. Tall cottonwoods line most sections, affording shade in the summer and a splash of bright color in the fall.

The trail is used by people on horseback, bikers, joggers, mothers with strollers, and those enjoying an environmental interlude. As parents amble leisurely, children run freely, hiding behind trees, chasing squirrels and birds darting across their paths.

The entire trail is wheelchair accessible, however curb cuts are not provided at every street crossing. During inclement weather, the 19-mile section of the trail south of Hampden Avenue is not suitable for wheelchair use.

Magpies and meadowlarks are among the birds that alight on branches that canopy the trail. Squirrels sprinting up a tree trunk are common along the residential sections. Prairie dogs and pheasants have been sighted in the open areas. And geese and a variety of ducks flock to the reservoirs and lakes that the canal feeds.

Wading, swimming, boating, and fishing are not permitted along the High Line Canal.

2. Crown Hill Park Nature Preserve Trail

Location: Crown Hill Park
Type: Dayhike
Difficulty: Easy for children
Hikable: July–February
Hiking time: 0.3 mile, loop; or 6.5 miles, loop
Starting elevation: 5280 feet
High point: 5280 feet
Maps: Crown Hill Park, Jefferson County Open Space
Wheelchair accessible

Driving Directions: Between 26th and 32nd avenues, east of Kipling Street in Jefferson County. Parking and toilet facilities are available on 26th Street near the entrance to the wildlife refuge. A Crown Hill Park map is available at the trailhead.

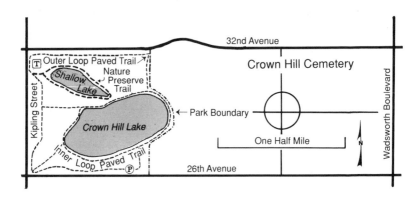

Nestled between two large suburban tracts, this wildlife refuge is as much an oasis for wildlife watchers as it is for the animals that migrate or live there. Crown Hill Park was dedicated on Earth Day 1990 as a Natural Urban Wildlife Sanctuary, and it more than lives up to its commitment. Established in 1981 as a joint project of the Jefferson County Open Space Program and the cities of Wheat Ridge and Lakewood, the park consists of a shallow pond and lake situated on 168 acres. Joggers, walkers, and people on horseback frequent the 6.5 miles of trails that circle the park and the lake.

The Nature Preserve Trail winds around the wildlife refuge, which is located in the park's northwest section. Here, the marsh habitat of Shallow Lake draws a variety of nesting birds and wildlife. During the peak nesting period, March 1 to June 30, the area is protected from human visitation. Horseback riders and pets are not allowed in the preserve even during the open visitation month. These regulations have allowed Crown Hill to become a wildlife watcher's paradise.

Blackbirds, the red-winged and yellow-headed types, are frequently seen perched on a reed above water. Look for their nests, a woven cup fastened to the tall grasses. A variety of ducks (red-headed and canvasbacks) and geese stop over here, and great blue herons frequent the pond's shores.

Blowing "seed angels" to the clouds

The area also supports turtles, bullfrogs, squirrels, skunks, foxes, and mule deer.

As of spring 1991, Shallow Lake will be edged by a 0.3-mile wheelchair-accessible boardwalk, which will circle the lake and wind through the cattails with several bird blinds along the way.

3. Niedrach Nature Trail and Gazebo Boardwalk

Location:	Barr Lake State Park
Type:	Dayhike
Difficulty:	Easy for children
Hikable:	March–November
Distance:	0.25 mile, loop, on Niedrach Nature Trail; 1.5 miles, one way, on Gazebo Boardwalk
Starting elevation:	5100 feet
High point:	5100 feet
Map:	Barr Lake State Park brochure
Wheelchair accessible	

Driving Directions: Located northeast of Denver. Take I-76 to Bromley Lane (Exit 22) for 1.8 miles to Picadilly Road, turn

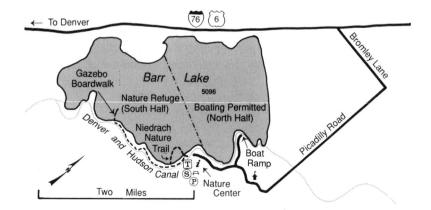

Boardwalk along Barr Lake

south. Proceed 1.9 miles to the park entrance and pay state park fee. Camping is not permitted here and swimming, dogs, or boats are prohibited from the southern half of the lake where the nature refuge is located.

Home to the only pair of nesting bald eagles on Colorado's Front Range, Barr Lake State Park offers a pleasant dayhike along a prairie reservoir. Opportunities for watching the hundreds of water birds that stop over, nest, or stay here are provided by a boardwalk and a gazebo situated in prime viewing areas. Kids love to use binoculars to watch the large birds take off and land on the water.

Before beginning the hike, stop at the nature center, a 0.25-mile drive southwest of the park's headquarters. Throughout the week, wildlife programs and guided walks begin here, free of charge. The center's naturalist will tell of recent bird sightings.

From the parking lot at the nature center, walk across the bridge over the Denver & Hudson Canal and turn left onto the Niedrach Nature Trail. Named for Robert Niedrach, an ornithologist who studied the birds of Barr Lake, this 0.25-mile boardwalk meanders through a cottonwood and willow marsh along the lake's eastern shore. The nature refuge, which is the lake's southern half, also begins here. Along the nature trail boardwalk, children enjoy stopping at the viewing stand to watch the large grebes, white pelicans, and great blue herons that frequent these waters. Grebes can be identified by their long, swan-like necks, which are white underneath. If you plan your Barr Lake visit for late May or early June, the grebes will be performing their mating dance—a well-choreographed ritual of the male and female birds crossing their necks then running across the water in synchrony with each other. The Niedrach Nature Trail loops back to the trail along the canal that meets the bridge.

Opposite the canal trail, a meadow of tall grasses reaches the horizon. On windy days, point out how the grasses move like waves on water. The shallow bay along here has several park benches nestled under the cottonwoods—perfect for viewing the ducks (mallards, pintails, teal) that patrol these waters.

If a chance to see bald eagles is a priority, your group will want to continue its walk 1 mile farther to the Gazebo Board-walk, which extends 950 feet out over the lake. Remind eager eagle watchers to approach the gazebo as quietly as possible. At this overlook, double-crested cormorants, white pelicans, and snowy egrets are among the birds dotting the waters of the surrounding heron rookery. Bald eagles raise their young here in the summer, but are seen throughout the year in this region.

Return by the same route.

Picnic, toilet, and water facilities are available at the nature center.

4. Red Rocks Trail

Location:	Mathews-Winters Park
Type:	Dayhike
Difficulty:	Moderate for children
Hikable:	Year-round
Distance:	2.5 miles, one way
Starting elevation:	6360 feet
High point:	6680 feet
Maps:	Mathews-Winters Park, Jefferson County Open Space

Driving Directions: Mathews-Winters Park may be reached by exiting I-70 on Exit 259 (Morrison). Head south under I-70 for 0.25 mile, taking the first road to the west (right), which leads to

A golden-mantled ground squirrel in Rocky Mountain National Park

the parking lot for the park's picnic area and access to the Village Walk Trail. To avoid an uphill backtrack, shuttle a car to the parking lot on the Red Rocks Loop Road, 2 miles south of CO-26.

A stroll through an historic town site followed by flower-dappled meadows with panoramic views of the region's alluring geology makes the Red Rocks Trail an ideal venture for the entire family.

Begin the trail at Mathews-Winters Park where the Village Walk loops around the site of the original boomtown of Mount Vernon. Gold miners lived here more than 100 years ago. Point out the miners' route to the goldfields of Central City—where CO-26 now bisects the valley below.

Access to the Red Rocks Trail is at the Village Walk Trail just beyond the picnic area across from Mount Vernon Creek. Take Village Walk Trail 0.3 mile up the gently sloping meadow, continuing to the hilltop scattered with gravestones. Engraved with names and dates as early as 1860, the headstones of this cemetery are all that remain of Mount Vernon. Children may have their own explanations for the few unnamed wooden grave markers among the headstones. The Red Rocks Trail meets the Village Walk just 0.1 mile beyond here.

Bordering the foothills that rise to the Front Range, the trail crosses open meadows and dips into a lush streambed at 1.2 miles as it descends into the valley. Chokecherry, wild plum, and willows thriving alongside the stream provide a shaded snack stop at several locations along this sun-exposed trail.

In the summer months, the children can have a field day learning about wildflowers; I identified more than 40 different bloomers during my late June visit. Bring a flower guide, but realize that young children may have more fun counting blue flowers or finding their favorite, or the "teeniest," or the biggest, or the prettiest smelling... rather than learning the names of different varieties.

Those with geologic curiosity should look toward the east at the ridge of yellow-white Dakota sandstone blocks tilted on edge. This formation is called a "hogback." Remind the football fan in your group that the Arkansas razorback is a fierce hog (boar) with armor-like plates along its spine, an image similar to the geologic barrier to the east.

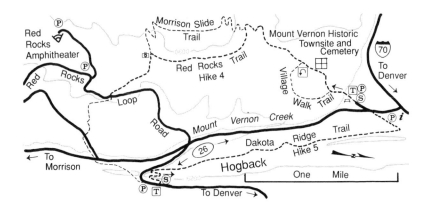

Lower Cathedral Lake

After passing the Morrison Slide spur at Cherry Gulch (about 1.2 miles), the trail enters into the red sandstone outcrops of the Fountain Formation. Within 0.7 mile, hikers reach a red rock overlook (and the opposite end of the Slide Trail). Then the trail heads east, briefly traversing Denver's Red Rocks Park before it crosses the road to Red Rocks Amphitheater. Most of the group can wait in the meadow here while the driver walks an additional 0.5 mile on the trail leading south and west to the parking area.

Picnic, toilet, and water facilities and a map are available. Camping is not allowed.

5. Dakota Ridge Trail

Location: Hogback Park
Type: Dayhike
Difficulty: Moderate for children
Hikable: April–November
Distance: 2 miles, one way
Starting elevation: 6360 feet
High point: 6640 feet
Maps: Mathews-Winters Park,
Jefferson County Open Space

Driving Directions: Heading west on I-70, take the Morrison exit (Exit 259) and turn south on CO-26. After passing under I-70, take the second left into the parking lot, which has a sign marked "geologic interest." The north end of the parking lot leads to an interpreted geologic walk along a road cut through the "hog-

Young investigators on their hands and knees at Dakota Hogback

back," while the southern end leads to the trailhead for the Dakota Ridge Trail. If a trail map is not available here, check at Mathews-Winters Park across the highway.

Walking along what a 12-year-old called "a stegosaurus backbone" is indeed a step into geologic history. The trail topping the Dakota Ridge, a spine of rocks tilted on edge just west of Denver in Hogback Park, offers sweeping views of Green Mountain Park and the Mile High City to the east, the plains to the south, and the foothills of the Rocky Mountains to the west. Thousand-year-old junipers offer occasional shade.

Hikers starting their walk at the north end of the hogback formation may wish to take the short walk north of the parking lot where geologic information signs are posted describing the formation of Dakota Ridge. Knowing that the exposed rocks of this ridge were formed 120 to 140 million years ago, a time when dinosaurs slogged through this once swampy area, will add special meaning to the hike. When children look closely at the hogback's rock ridges they will discover they are made of sand compressed very tightly. Ask them from where they think the sand came.

Begin the Dakota Ridge walk at the southern end of the parking lot where an old road leads to the crest of the hogback. From this point, the trail snakes its way south traversing up and over several tilted ridges or hogbacks.

When the trail reaches its highest point at about 0.8 mile, look to the east for views of Green Mountain Park, a 1200-acre bundle of wilderness bordering the city of Lakewood. Also in that direction, Denver erupts from the plains like a magic kingdom. To the west are green-sloped foothills and Mount Morrison. As your hikers weave in and around the imposing boulders of this trail, have them explain why the junipers clinging to the sandy soil appear twisted and old. (As grown-ups know, wind, sun, and time are quite effective at aging.)

As the trail reaches its southern end, follow a switchback 0.2 mile down the hogback's east side to cross CO-26. Limited parking is available along the east side of the highway for those who have shuttled their vehicle to the trail's end. If you don't have a car at the end of the trail, return the way you came for a total trip of 4 miles.

Picnic, toilet, and water facilities are available across the highway at Mathews-Winters Park.

6. Meadow View Trail

Location: Elk Meadow Park
Type: Dayhike
Difficulty: Moderate for children
Hikable: April–November
Distance: 3.3 miles, one way
Starting elevation: 7760 feet
High point: 8110 feet
Maps: Elk Meadow Park, Jefferson County Open Space

Driving Directions: Parking for Elk Meadow's north entrance is 4.7 miles north of Evergreen (or 0.1 mile south of Evergreen Junior High) on CO-74. Parking and the trailhead, where a map is available, are on the west side of the road.

A grassy meadow peppered with wildflowers and edged in pine forests is but one reason the Meadow View Trail in Elk Meadow Park appeals to all ages. Elk and deer often browse its open grasslands, while a variety of birds and the tassel-eared squirrel make their homes in the trail's ponderosa pine and fir

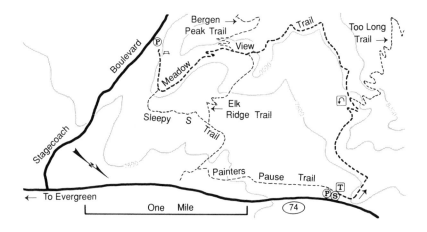

Irises capture a toddler's interest at Elk Meadow Park.

forests. Also, the fact that Elk Meadow Park is located close to the city of Evergreen makes this an even more desirable destination.

 Starting from the north parking lot, the trail gently climbs across a meadow before entering a pine forest. Traffic noise subsides here, giving way to bird calls. Young hikers will notice shiny bits of rock speckling the trail. Called mica, this mineral can be easily separated into paper-thin, almost transparent flakes. Ask the kids how the glass-like mineral may have been used "in the old days."

 Within 1 mile, the trail meets Too Long Trail near a shady site that can serve as a destination for easily tired hikers. Continue walking southwest, crossing dry and wet creek beds and dipping in and out of the forest.

While traversing a stand of fir trees (those with flat and flexible needles), ask the kids to find north by watching for trees with moss growing on one side of the trunk. Once they've determined south, east, and west, make up a game in which each hiker names the direction each time the trail turns sharply.

Many types of wildlife find food and shelter in the forest edge. The resident elk herd is seen in the open meadows here during the winter when snow in the high altitudes sends them lower. Perhaps someone will see the nest of a tassel-eared Abert squirrel built in the crotch of a ponderosa pine.

Shortly after meeting Elk Ridge Trail at 2.1 miles, the trail descends gradually through aspens for 0.2 mile where it meets Bergen Peak Trail. Head east on Meadow View Trail for 0.7 mile until the Sleepy "S" Trail joins it. The final 0.3-mile stretch heads westerly to the parking lot at the Elk Meadow Park south entrance on Stagecoach Boulevard.

Groups can avoid backtracking by leaving a car at the park's south parking lot, 1.2 miles west on Stagecoach Boulevard, which is 2.7 miles north of Evergreen on CO-74.

Picnic, toilet, and water facilities are available only at the south entrance to Elk Meadow Park.

7. Meadow–Castle Loop

Location:	Mount Falcon Park
Type:	Dayhike
Difficulty:	Easy for children
Hikable:	March–November
Distance:	1.8 miles, loop; plus several longer options
Starting elevation:	7750 feet
High point:	7800 feet
Maps:	Mount Falcon Park, Jefferson County Open Space

Driving Directions: From US 285 near Evergreen take CO-8 west for 2.5 miles to the Indian Hills/Parmalee Gulch Road (Road 120). Turn east and travel 2.7 miles on this paved road to the Mount Falcon turnoff on the right. Continue watching for Mount Falcon Park signs as the gravel roadway climbs nearly 1000 feet over 2 winding miles to the park's west boundary and parking area.

A peaceful walk through meadows to a mountaintop castle is what dreams are made of—and few hikers on the Meadow and Castle trails can resist dreaming of an equally grand palace to re-

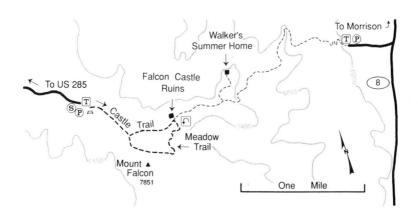

place the remains of John B. Walker's palatial home that briefly crested Mount Falcon.

Start the Meadow–Castle Loop from Mount Falcon Park's west parking lot. From here, take the Castle Trail, which crosses a flower-speckled field for 0.4 mile before it meets the Meadow Trail. This smooth, wide walkway contours the grassland's edge and dips into the trees for 0.5 mile then turns north crossing an open meadow before it reconnects to the Castle Trail. The crumbling remnants of Walker's dream are perched on a ridge just north of this intersection.

Although broken stone walls and charred fireplaces are all that remain of Walker's magnificent house, the views of the plains to the east and mountains to the west must have fueled his inspiration. Here, kids are prone to pretend. I watched three nine-year-olds stoically guard this mighty fortress, then capture it as reckless bandits.

For a look at another grandiose plan of this diversely talented entrepreneur, walk 0.8 mile east of this point to the spot where the foundation of Walker's summer home for U.S. presidents sits on a ridge. Construction on the Summer White House started in 1918, but when Walker's home was struck and destroyed by lightning, and then his beautiful young wife died suddenly and several business ventures failed, his plans were dropped. In 1931, he died penniless at the age of 83. From the Summer White House site, point out to your children one of Walker's dreams that came true: Red Rocks Park.

To return to the parking lot and complete the 1.8-mile loop, head west from Walker's home ruins on the Castle Trail.

The variety of trails in this park provides options for easy dayhikes and more demanding ventures. The Castle Trail can be hiked 4 miles downhill from the west to the east parking lot if one car is left at each end.

Picnic, toilet, and water facilities and a map are available at the trailhead.

The remains of Walker's castle

8. South Rim Trail

Location:	Roxborough State Park
Type:	Dayhike
Difficulty:	Moderate for children
Hikable:	March–mid-November
Distance:	3.5 miles, loop
Starting elevation:	6200 feet
High point:	6400 feet
Map:	Roxborough State Park brochure

Driving Directions: Roxborough State Park is located south of Denver and south of Chatfield Reservoir. From I-470, exit at CO-85/Santa Fe Road and travel south for 4.9 miles to Titan Road. Head west for 3.4 miles where the road bends south and continues as Rampart Road for 3.3 miles until the gravel road turnoff to Roxborough Community Center. Drive 2.25 miles to the park entrance and pay an admission fee. As a National Natural Landmark, this park protects its unparalleled scenery by prohibiting camping, pets, and climbing on the rocks.

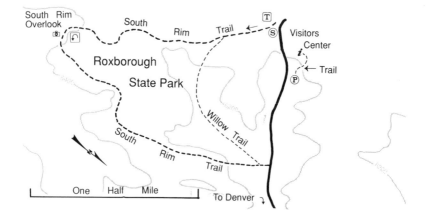

The Fountain Formation of Roxborough State Park

Less than an hour's drive from Denver, Roxborough State Park offers visitors a look at more than 1.2 billion years of geologic time spread across a variety of pristine habitats. Mule deer, coyotes, and squirrels are common sights here, and bobcat and elk make occasional appearances. Watchful visitors often see a golden eagle circling overhead. The best way to sample this unspoiled enclave of nature is via the South Rim Trail, the park's newest trail since 1989.

For an informed walk through the park's geologic display, and to learn the flora and fauna that frequent the trails, start at the visitor center. Numerous displays, movies, and lectures explaining these features are available.

Access to the South Rim Trail is the Willow Trail, 100 yards north of the visitor center. Walking in the shade of scrub oak, hik-ers notice the unique blend of prairie and mountain plants such as plains cactus and yucca sharing the ground with aspen and wild rose. But as the climb to the rim begins at 1.2 miles, your kids will pay more attention to the spectacular rock formations of the park.

The iron-stained red rock wedges of the Fountain Formation erupt from the valley's green foliage like a giant stegosaurus crawling through lush vegetation. The light-yellow ridge east of it is the Lyons Formation—once a series of stream deposits and sand dunes along ancient seas. The next rock formation, the Dakota Hogback Ridge, is composed of sandstone deposited as flood plains 120 to 140 million years ago. At the south rim overlook (1.5 miles), your children can see the distinct colors of these rows of tilted boulders. As the Rocky Mountains rose, 70 million years ago, these formations also tilted upward.

The views at your feet can be equally unforgettable here—

Hollywood coils in defense.

especially if they consist of a prairie rattler, sometimes seen in this protected natural resource. Perhaps your group will meet "Hollywood," the name given to the prairie rattler often seen near the visitor center. From a safe distance (3 yards or more) you can see its rattles at the end of its tail, a series of horny interlocking segments. A new rattle forms when the snake sheds its skin, two to four times a year. Though not aggressive, vipers rattle and assume a coiled, defensive position if approached. If left alone, they crawl away and hide.

Also, keep a safe distance from the patches of poison ivy that grace a few of the park's trails, but take a moment to show children the characteristic dark green, shiny leaves of poison ivy. The wooden benches along the trail are intended to protect you and the fragile environment.

From the rim, the trail descends 1.3 miles across an open slope to the park's access road. From here, the trail parallels the road through meadow grasses for 0.5 mile before returning to the visitor center parking lot.

Water and toilet facilities are available only at the visitor center.

---

9. Horseshoe Trail to Frazer Meadow

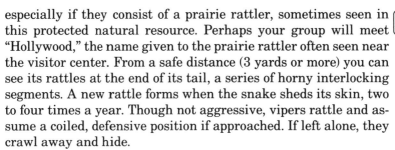

Location:	Golden Gate State Park
Type:	Dayhike or backpack
Difficulty:	Moderate for children
Hikable:	June–mid-October
Distance:	2 miles, one way
Starting elevation:	8100 feet
High point:	9050 feet
Maps:	Golden Gate State Park, USGS Blackhawk

Driving Directions: From downtown Golden, head 1.5 miles northwest on CO-93 to Golden Gate Canyon Road, turn left. Proceed 13 miles to the visitor center of Golden Gate State Park. You will need to pay an admission fee. (Check here for information about nature walks and Saturday programs, and to obtain required backcountry camping permits.) Parking is available at the Frazer Meadow trailhead, located 0.3 mile northeast of the visitor center.

Birdsong and a babbling brook accompany hikers along this pleasant journey through an aspen- and pine-fringed meadow that leads to a homesteader's cabin. Children will want to explore the tall grass surrounding the cabin in search of forgotten horse-drawn farm equipment.

At the Frazer Meadow trailhead, the trail begins its 850-foot gradual climb in an aspen-shaded forest paralleling a creek. Have kids watch for the horseshoe sign marking trees along the trail. Tell them they will cross the creek four times before reaching Frazer Meadow.

At 1.2 miles, a spur trail on the right leads to primitive camp-sites in Greenfield Meadow (homesteaded by the Greenfield family). No fires are allowed in these and other backcountry campsites in the park. Beyond here, the trail crosses the creek

The Frazer Meadow homestead

and enters a lodgepole and ponderosa pine forest before it meets
the Ground Squirrel Trail on the left at 1.5 miles. Stop to compare
the two pines: the differences in needle length, the smell and size
of trunk, and the shape of the cones. Ponderosa needles grow in
bundles of two to three and are 3 to 9 inches long, while lodgepole
needles come in pairs, 1 to 3 inches long. Continue following the
Horseshoe Trail to the right (northwest) as the leaves of the
young aspen trees seem to applaud your passage.

The last creek crossing leads to the open meadow where John
and Rufus Frazer built their log cabin and barn in the 1880s. The
brothers raised cattle here, earning extra cash by cutting and
hauling timber. Perhaps the cart used to carry the logs down the
valley can be found among the homestead remnants. Visitors are
asked not to climb or enter the historical structure.

The meadow is the turnaround point for the 4-mile total hike.
Those planning an extended hike can join one of three trails that
intersect at the log cabin and barn.

During the return walk, listen for the whirring buzz of the
broad-tailed hummingbird, identified by its iridescent green back
and red throat. Frequently seen darting above meadows in the
Rocky Mountains, this flying ace cannot walk or glide but will
perch for a moment on a bare limb of an aspen. If a female hum-
mer is in the vicinity, you may be able to watch the tiny male bird
in its courtship dance, looping straight upward then down and
around, as if it were on an invisible roller coaster.

Toilet facilities are located at the visitor center.

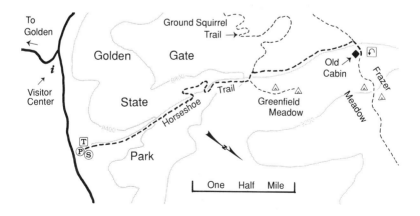

10. Enchanted Mesa–McClintock Nature Trail

Location: Boulder
Type: Dayhike
Difficulty: Easy for children
Hikable: March–November
Distance: 1.8 miles, loop
Starting elevation: 5800 feet
High point: 6160 feet
Maps: City of Boulder Open Space
Trails, Boulder Mountain Park
Trail map from Colorado
Mountain Club, USGS Boulder
Wheelchair accessible for the first mile

Driving Directions: From CO-93 (Broadway), head west on Baseline to Twelfth Street, turn left. Follow this road until it ends behind the Chautauqua Auditorium. Park at the picnic shelter.

This easily accessible loop trail treats hikers to quiet views of the towering Flatirons, a walk through a pine forest, and a ramble along a diversely vegetated stream. Interpretive signs on the McClintock section encourage children to look, touch, and discover. No bicycles are allowed on this trail—a refreshing experience in a city where bicycles seem to outnumber cars.

Beginning at the picnic pavilion, the Enchanted Mesa

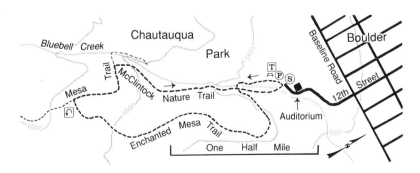

The rings on this tree stump show how old it is.

(wheelchair accessible) Trail veers east (left) on a 12-foot-wide pathway offering views of the Boulder valley. As the trail heads south, look skyward for the red cliffs of the Flatirons.

Formed 250 million years ago, the Flatirons are like great-grandfathers to the nearby mountains. These ancestors to the Rocky Mountain range were uplifted and eroded 200 million years before the present "Rockies" were formed. Their red color indicates the presence of iron. Children will be surprised to learn that the Flatirons may have been as high as our Rocky Mountains are now. Ask what caused the Flatirons to get smaller. (Erosion caused by wind, rain, and ice.)

At 0.8 mile, as the trail enters a ponderosa pine stand, your children will notice this forest has been thinned; 12-foot-high tree stumps share the forest floor with the season's wildflowers. Kids can estimate the age of this forest by counting the number of branches along one side of the trunk. (This method works best on trees 4 to 10 feet tall. A more accurate technique, one that requires kneeling close to a stump, is to count the tree rings, starting from the center.)

Within 1 mile, at the top of a gentle slope in the pine forest, the Enchanted Mesa Trail joins the Mesa Trail (which is not wheelchair accessible) for 0.3 mile before the McClintock Nature Trail begins. This 20-station self-guided nature walk is named for an avid conservationist and former advisory member of Boulder's Park Board.

Paralleling Bluebell Creek, the trail enters a diversely vegetated region, rich with birdsong. Ask your companions to find tree trunks dimpled by woodpeckers that have drilled holes in search of a beetle or ant. Explain that these wood-boring birds use their long tongues to stab an insect and pull it from the hole. Their diet is an important means of controlling insect infestation in the forest.

When the McClintock Trail meets the wider pathway of Enchanted Mesa, jog right 10 yards to walk the final 0.2 mile through tall grasses, ending at the trailhead/picnic area.

Toilet and water facilities are available at the Chautauqua Auditorium.

11. Betasso Preserve Canyon Loop

Location:	Betasso Preserve
Type:	Dayhike
Difficulty:	Moderate for children
Hikable:	May–October
Distance:	2.8 miles, loop
Starting elevation:	6540 feet
High point:	7420 feet
Maps:	Betasso Preserve brochure, Boulder County Parks & Open Space

Driving Directions: Betasso Preserve is 6 miles west of Boulder off Sugarloaf Road. The park is open from sunrise to sunset.

This vigorous trail crosses flowered fields, a lush stream bed, a dense forest, and a meadow as it loops around the junction of Boulder and Fourmile canyons. Families with little ones will enjoy the easy climb to and across a meadow at the trail's beginning, and older kids will steam ahead to explore the changing terrain.

Begin the trek on the old farm road heading northeast from the Betasso Preserve parking lot. In 0.5 mile, turn right on the

Forest finds are for feeling.

narrow trail traversing a meadow. This is an ideal destination for
very young hikers.

This land was not homesteaded until 1912, three years later
becoming a cattle ranch operated by the Betasso family. Now operated by Boulder County Parks & Open Space, Betasso Preserve
features deer instead of cows. If your hike takes place in the early
morning or evening, you have a good chance of seeing a small
group of deer feed.

Throughout the day, the area's bird choir gives a free concert,
telling each other where food can be found or warning of human
presence. Encourage the children to listen for two birds communi-
cating.

At 1 mile, the trail dips down the canyon ravine. Kids will
notice chunks of pink and white quartz rocks sprinkling the
ground. These are examples of the oldest rocks in Boulder
County—Boulder Creek granodiorite. This 1.7-billion-year-old
rock was formed from molten material. Your school-age companions can tell you that the rocks are igneous.

Newly formed cones of a ponderosa pine

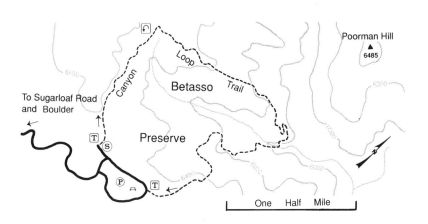

Within a steep 0.5-mile descent, the trail meets a stream bordered by a thick variety of trees. This small area, considered a riparian zone, is an important source of food, water, and shelter for the area's birds and mammals. (Seventy percent of the state's wildlife depends on riparian zones, yet only 3 percent of the state is classified as such.) Enter this area quietly, asking youngsters to watch for animals using this habitat. Birds alighting on tree branches, water striders skimming across the creek, bees feeding on flowers, or a spider spinning a web may be among their finds.

Enjoy a cool rest in the shade here—it's a serious climb up and out of the canyon. However, within 0.5 mile the trail becomes level as it crosses an open hilltop. Views of the surrounding slopes and canyons are excellent here. Continue hiking south as the trail winds past a picnic site and returns to the parking lot.

Toilet and picnic facilities are available.

12. Pine to Peak Trail

Location:	Bald Mountain Scenic Area
Type:	Dayhike
Difficulty:	Easy for children
Hikable:	Year-round
Distance:	1 mile, loop
Starting elevation:	6960 feet
High point:	7160 feet
Maps:	Bald Mountain Scenic Area brochure, Boulder County Parks & Open Space, USGS Gold Hill

Driving Directions: From Boulder, take Ninth Street to Sunshine Canyon Drive. Turn west and proceed 5 miles to the parking lot for the Bald Mountain Scenic Area on the south side of the road.

Requiring little effort, yet offering magnificent views, a hike up Bald Mountain can be the first "peak" for beginning mountain climbers.

The trail to this barren, windswept mountaintop begins in the friendly confines of a ponderosa pine forest adjacent to the parking lot. While walking through this forest, alert children to the rhythmical tapping of a hairy woodpecker, or the chatter of tassel-eared Abert squirrels, both residents here. Your youngsters may see a stout gray bird climbing headfirst down the pine trees. This acrobat is a nuthatch, either a pygmy or white-breasted variety.

Contouring the base of Bald Mountain, the trail heads west 0.3 mile into an open grassland where the wildflowers at your feet are as spectacular as the views of snow-covered mountaintops on the horizon. Equally important, though far less glamorous, are the grasses that blanket the slope. During the next rest stop, ask your young hikers to find two or three grass varieties. Unlike many wildflowers, grasses grow in tight clumps, holding the minimal soil here in place. For kids, however, grasses are better suited as tickling wands or as whistles between their thumbs!

As the trail loops around and heads south, watch for the short spur trail on the right, 0.4 mile, that leads to a throne of rocks; a perfect seat for assessing the views. A ponderosa pine tree, securely rooted in the rubble, seems to like this spot also. A picnic table overlooking the west is near here.

In less than 0.5 mile, the High Plains Overlook Trail intersects the main trail to the summit. Boulder valley, Denver, and beyond can be seen at this point. Those who prefer a less strenuous walk to the parking lot should take this trail to the right. The

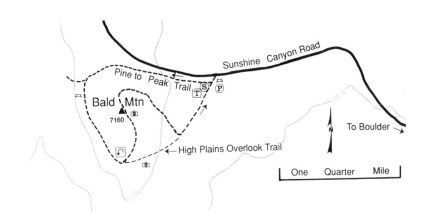

Peak climbers enjoy the views from Bald Mountain.

"summit" is on your left, only a short walk up the hill.

Few trees survive at the top of Bald Mountain, hence its name. Close inspection of the soil shows that it is composed of tiny rocks. Your children may point out other factors, such as steep terrain, hot summer sun, and cold winter winds, that prevent trees from taking root on this mountaintop.

To return to the parking lot, follow the trail down the opposite side of the mountain. No toilet or water facilities are available here.

13. Rattlesnake Gulch Trail

Location:	Eldorado State Park
Type:	Dayhike
Difficulty:	Moderate for children
Hikable:	May–October
Distance:	1.4 miles, one way
Starting elevation:	6050 feet
High point:	6760 feet
Maps:	Eldorado Canyon State Park brochure, USGS Eldorado Springs

Driving Directions: Eldorado Canyon State Park can be reached from Eldorado Springs via CO-170, 3 miles west of CO-93 (Broadway). The last 0.3 mile is a gravel road that passes the pool/resort area. Travel 1 mile west of the entrance, at which you'll need to pay an admission fee, and cross the bridge over South Boulder Creek to the visitor center.

Exploring the remains of a luxury hotel perched on a canyon promontory is just one reason to walk this popular trail in

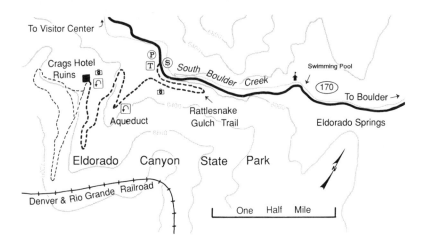

Rock climbers rappel from the cliffs at Eldorado Canyon.

Eldorado State Park. Rock climbers clinging to 1000-foot sand-stone walls, views of the Continental Divide, and a chance to see a still-in-use historic railroad line 500 feet overhead are among the attractions on the Rattlesnake Gulch trail.

The trailhead is on the right side of the road 0.5 mile south-west of the visitor center. From here, it traverses the canyon wall above and across South Boulder Creek, a white foaming current that slices through the narrow canyon. Initially, the trail winds through a boulder-strewn path then edges close to open cliff sides—youngsters who tend to wander need to be reined in here.

Following the canyon contours, at 0.4 mile, the trail nears a 10-foot-wide cement aqueduct carrying water from South Boulder Creek to Denver. Have children place their hand on the pipe to feel and hear the water rushing past. The meadow area around here could serve as a destination for younger hikers.

When the rumble of a train is heard, look up—the Denver & Rio Grande is riding the rails laid at the turn of the century for the Moffat Railroad line.

As the trail continues climbing the canyon for 1 more mile, the views of Eldorado Springs and the sheer rock walls of the park loom grandly. Binoculars are useful here for watching rock climb-ers scale the precipitous cliffs.

The remains of the Crags Hotel, a short-lived luxury resort, lie in stone and brick pieces on the grassy promontory at 1.4 miles. Beginning in 1908, guests arrived above here via the Mof-fat Railroad, then took a burro and buggy ride to the hotel. Young detectives in your group will enjoy finding what's left of the hotel's fireplaces, garden pools, and even fountains. Fire de-stroyed the hotel in 1912. Turn around and head back at this point.

For another view of the canyon, the Continental Divide, (looking west), and access to the same path the hotel guests once used, continue following the trail 0.3 mile through a forested hill-side. The railroad line will appear above 250 feet on the left just before the viewpoint.

Return is via the same trail. Water, toilet, and picnic facili-ties are available at the visitor center.

14. Garden of the Gods
Central Garden Zone Trail

Location:	Garden of the Gods
Type:	Dayhike
Difficulty:	Easy for children
Hikable:	Year-round
Distance:	0.6 mile, loop
Starting elevation:	6450 feet
High point:	6460 feet
Map:	Garden of the Gods brochure
Wheelchair accessible	

Driving Directions: From I-25 South in Colorado Springs, head west on US 24 to Exit 141 to Ridge Road. Proceed 2.7 miles north, past the Garden of the Gods entrance, to the Hidden Inn Trading Post parking lot. Watch for the trail sign opposite the parking lot at the bottom of the hill. At the park's visitor center, you can pick up a brochure that contains a map of the area.

A garden walk among the park's most stunning red rock spires is what you can expect from this paved, wheelchair-accessible trail. Several side trails lead directly to the unusual rock formations, giving children a firsthand feel of history eons before the dinosaurs arrived.

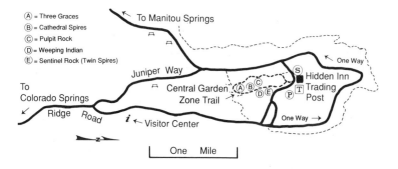

The 300-million-year-old sentinels at Garden of the Gods

At the trailhead near Hidden Inn, turn left. Here the panorama of rock formations begins. Children's imaginations are teased by the shapes they see in the rocks. One youngster may describe Weeping Indian rock as "a pirate's ship pulling a dinghy," another may see it as a "school bus with wings."

For those interested in knowing the real names of the 300-million-year-old formations they pass, the first set of slender twin spires is called Sentinel Rock, followed by a massive shape called Weeping Indian. At the top of the loop (0.3 mile), Cathedral Spires consists of three cone shapes, followed by Three Graces.

Pulpit Rock stands alone in the grassy area of the loop. Snow-capped Pikes Peak is an impressive backdrop for photographs taken here.

Equally impressive to the park's unique geologic display, though far less obvious, is the blend of life zones and ecosystems. Juniper trees, characteristic of the Southwest, converge with the fir and spruce trees of the mountain forest and grasses of the Great Plains.

Point out the small blue berries on the juniper. Children are surprised to learn that American Indians ate them raw. They also cooked, dried, and ground the bitter, dry fruits into a flour or a flavoring used for a coffee-like drink. Most grown-ups know that juniper berries are the flavoring in gin. During times of survival, Indians stripped off and chewed the tree's inner bark. Nowadays, its durable, moisture-resistant trunk is used for fence posts.

Rock climbers, carefully scaling the park's summits, capture the interest of many children. Detours along the Garden Zone Trail provide several opportunities for children to scale safe rocks. Please stay on marked trails. The area has been replanted with native grasses and shrubs to control erosion.

Toilet and water facilities are available at the trailhead and at the park's visitor center.

15. Columbine Trail

Location:	North Cheyenne Cañon
Type:	Dayhike
Difficulty:	Easy for children
Hikable:	March–November
Distance:	3 miles, one way
Starting elevation:	7300 feet
High point:	7500 feet
Maps:	North Cheyenne Cañon brochure, USGS Manitou Springs

Driving Directions: From 21st/Cresta and CO-24, travel south 3 miles to Cheyenne Boulevard. Turning west, drive 1 mile through a suburban neighborhood to the North Cheyenne Cañon Park entrance. (Entry to Seven Falls is on the left.) Parking for the upper Columbine trailhead is 2.8 miles (or 0.1 mile beyond Helen Hunt Visitor Center) west of the park entrance. Hikers completing the 3-mile walk down the canyon can be picked up at the small parking area near the mid-Columbine Trail sign located 1.8 miles from the upper Columbine trailhead.

The Columbine Trail offers a perfect solution for groups of eager trailblazers mixed with not-so-certain toddlers: While one adult and the youngsters explore the Helen Hunt Falls area near the trailhead, another adult can lead hikers down the Columbine Trail. At a prearranged time, say, 1.5 hours, the adult with the waterfall explorers drives to Columbine Trail's midpoint, where the group reunites.

From its trailhead, the Columbine Trail climbs the hillside via three short switchbacks before overlooking the Helen Hunt and Silver Cascade falls. The promontory at 0.4 mile offers views of Colorado Springs and the plains beyond while serving as a destination for a shorter hike. Although the trail is well graded, hold on to youngsters who may be quick to dart off; the trail runs along steep, open, and gravelly terrain.

Following the canyon's contours, the trail descends through forests of pinyon, spruce, and Douglas fir until it crosses a dry creek and climbs to another viewpoint at 1.6 miles. Here I heard a young hiker say, "Is that Kansas out there?"

Stop to inspect those patches of bright green ivy called "kinnikinnick" that cling to the granite-laden soil of the canyon. Also

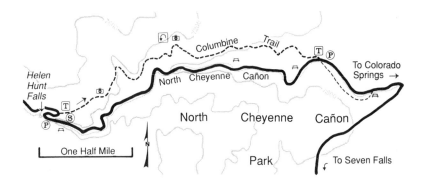

White phlox

called "manzanita" or "bearberry," this groundcover produces red berries favored by bears, deer, and birds. Its leaves have medicinal value and were used by Indians as a tobacco.

Signs of careless hikers cutting across switchbacks are evidenced in this rocky terrain where the meager vegetation has been stripped away leaving a barren, vertical path. Damage to delicate plant life such as this takes years to repair itself. Encourage slow, careful walking for the last mile; the loose gravel of this steep section is made up of pebbles, sometimes causing loose footing and skinned knees.

After crossing a small creek, the trail continues to descend, terminating in a massive red rock formation similar to those seen in Garden of the Gods.

16. Waldo Canyon Loop No. 640

Location:	Pike National Forest
Type:	Dayhike or backpack
Difficulty:	Moderate for children
Hikable:	April–November
Distance:	6.8 miles, loop
Starting elevation:	7020 feet
High point:	8000 feet
Maps:	Pike National Forest, USGS Cascade

Driving Directions: From Manitou Springs, take the US 24 bypass west for 2 miles. Watch for the parking area on the north side of the highway. A metal sign and stairway mark the beginning of the trail.

A loop trail offering views of Pikes Peak, a meandering stream, boulders for climbing, flowering cactus, and a variety of forests—what more could one ask for? Waldo Canyon Loop Trail combines all of these along with destinations that will suit the stature or time frame of any hiker.

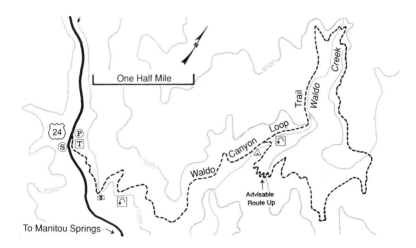

Pikes Peak dominates the views from Waldo Canyon.

Trail 640 climbs a ridge for 1.6 miles before it meets Waldo Canyon. Pikes Peak dominates the vista along most of the trail, but watch for the equally exquisite sights at your feet—spring flowering barrel cactus or the tracks of a bighorn sheep. At 0.6 mile, the trail leads to a boulder-filled overlook, which can serve as a shaded picnic destination or as a stop for young climbers to try their skills.

Children may want to inspect the gray-green lichen that crusts these and other boulders in the region. (A magnifying glass is fun to use here.) They'll be fascinated to know that lichen is actually a combination of two microscopic plants that are dependent on each other for survival. One plant in the partnership is an algae that produces sugars. The other is a fungus that produces an acid that breaks down the rock, providing mineral nutrients for both plants. Encourage the children to discover different varieties of lichen by discerning colors and textures.

From here, the trail descends gradually into Waldo Canyon. At 1.8 miles, the trail enters a clearing, formerly the site of the

Waldo Hog Ranch. Hot, tired feet can be cooled in Waldo Creek, which borders the trail. Numerous undeveloped camping sites dot this area. Just 0.1 mile beyond is the junction for the 3-mile loop portion of the trail.

For those planning to hike the entire loop, the route headed east is advised. After a steady climb up and around the canyon, the hiker is rewarded with magnificent views of Pikes Peak followed by a casual descent alongside a forest-shaded creek. If you choose to turn around here, first head west and enjoy the trail's streamside tranquillity.

No toilet, water, or picnic facilities are available here.

17. B.P.W. Nature Trail

Location: Pike National Forest
Type: Dayhike
Difficulty: Easy for children
Hikable: June–mid-October
Distance: 0.4 mile, loop
Starting elevation: 9160 feet
High point: 9180 feet
Map: Pike National Forest
Wheelchair accessible

Driving Directions: From CO-24 in Woodland Park, watch for the sign "to Rampart Road" east of McDonald's. Turn north and continue for 3 miles past a residential area. Turn right (east) at the fork. Go another 2.5 miles and turn right, traveling 5.5 miles following the signs for Rampart Reservoir. The parking lot for the B.P.W. Trail is on the left, just past the Thunder Ridge Campground.

This interpreted nature trail meanders through the most interesting forest ecosystems: a marshy creek, a sunny hillside, a gang of giant boulders, and a cool, wet coniferous forest. This trail was built by the Colorado Federation of Business and Professional Women's Clubs Inc. and the U.S. Forest Service. It is wheelchair accessible with signs, written in Braille and English, that encourage any hiker to stop, listen, feel, and discover. In addition, it's an ideal getaway for families vacationing at nearby Rampart Reservoir.

Just beyond the parking lot trailhead, a boardwalk takes hikers across a boggy creek. Self-planting willows, which reproduce when a branch is set in water, dominate the foliage here. Within a few yards the scene changes to a dry, sunny slope blanketed by thin-bladed grasses—an inviting spot for kids to lie down and watch birds circle overhead.

Notice the ropes of soil on top of the grasses here. Pocket gophers in search of food have left them. As gophers build their underground burrows, eating roots and seedlings along the way, they push loose mounds of earth to the top. (Twenty gophers will eat about 400 pounds of forage, mostly roots, in a year.) These rarely seen meadow miners carry soil in their fur-lined pouches on the outside of their cheeks. How does the fur lining help the gophers?

As the boardwalk winds around and between the granite boulders, children should feel and compare the moss and lichen clinging to the surface of the boulders. (Blindfolds are fun to use here.) They might describe the moss as soft and velvety while the lichen feels hard and scratchy.

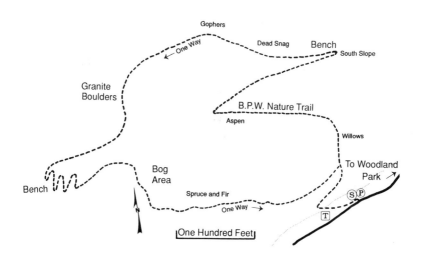

A hiker enters the gallery of boulders along the B.P.W. Nature Trail.

Forty yards from here the trail enters a north slope bog area, marked by the quiet trickle of a small stream. Watch for another, longer-haired moss clinging to the swatches of wet soil pulled up as tall pines have toppled over. A park bench is provided for quiet reflection here, but most youngsters will prefer exploring the many-channeled creek feeding this region. Muddy knees are inevitable on this hike!

Wheelchair-accessible toilet and water facilities are available at the trailhead.

18. The Crags Trail

Location:	Pike National Forest
Type:	Dayhike
Difficulty:	Moderate to challenging for children
Hikable:	Late May–mid-October
Distance:	2 miles, one way
Starting elevation:	10,040 feet
High point:	10,680 feet
Maps:	Pike National Forest, USGS Woodland Park, USGS Pikes Peak

Driving Directions: From Colorado Springs, travel west on CO-24 past Woodland Park to Divide Street (CO-67). Turn left (south) and proceed 4 miles to County Road 62 (Forest Road 383) and turn left. Drive 3.6 miles to Crags Campground; the trailhead is located just beyond the last campsite. A parking lot for hikers is on the right side of the road.

Children of all ages will discover rocks to climb, pinnacles to reach, and streams to investigate on this intriguing trail leading to what a 12-year-old companion called an "awesome" rock formation. Groups consisting of those with little legs and those with strong, eager ones will find a number of satisfying destinations along the way.

From the trailhead parking lot, the trail meanders through

aspen meadows fringed with pines. A clear and shallow gravel-bottomed creek accompanies hikers as they enter a marshy area at 0.3 mile. Look up here to see the trail's namesake—crags, a group of rock pinnacle formations on the horizon.

Entering a meadow at about 0.5 mile, point out to children the tangles of gray, fallen aspen trees on the left. Ask them what kind of tree is growing in place of the aspens. The answer is "pine trees" or spruce.

Continue walking another 0.7 mile northeast, where boulders rimming meadows on both sides of the trail increase in size and imagination-teasing shapes. Looking directly north, a horizon-high rock formation appears to be the crenellated walls of a castle and nearby is a giant palace of rocks. Ask children to describe what they see.

Along this boulder-studded region, a number of spur trails lead to rock walls. Climbers, new and seasoned, will want to try their finger- and toehold techniques on the cracks and fissures.

 At the base of these formations, enjoy a snack stop with the babbling creek nearby. While resting, point out the erosion of waist-high rocks. When children merely touch these boulders, quarter-inch pebbles crumble off, like snakes shedding skin. Perhaps they can estimate how long it takes these rocks to naturally erode into a pile of rubble.

At 1.5 miles, the trail reenters a forested area then climbs to an overlook of the area's reservoirs and forests. From here, the trail's last 0.2 mile to the promontory gets a bit hard to follow as it traverses a granite base. Keep heading west and uphill.

In this timberline region, twisted limber pines cling to life

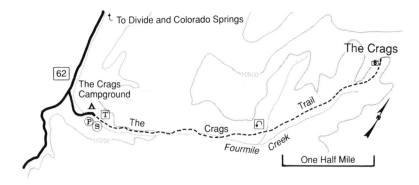

The Crags

between the boulders. Steady winds carrying snow and rain have
stunted these trees into unusual shapes. When kids discover the
bendable nature of the tree's thin branches, they'll know why the
tree is called "limber." At the promontory, they'll have 360-de-
gree views of mountains and valleys silhouetted by towering rock
pinnacles that rival those seen from Pikes Peak. A jacket may be
needed for this windy summit.

Return via the same route. Picnic, water, and toilet facilities
are available at Crags Campground.

19. Alpine Garden Loop and Mount Goliath Trails

Location:	Arapaho National Forest
Type:	Dayhike
Difficulty:	Easy for children
Hikable:	June to first snowfall
Distance:	0.5 mile, loop; or 1.1 miles, one way
Starting elevation:	12,140 feet
High point:	12,140 feet
Maps:	Arapaho National Forest, USGS Clear Creek, USGS Mount Evans

Driving Directions: From I-70 near Idaho Springs, take CO-103 south 10 miles to Echo Lake and its junction with the Mount Evans Highway (CO-5). Turn right and drive 4.8 miles to the Alpine Garden Loop trailhead on the left. Parking is adjacent to the highway. The Mount Evans Highway closes at the first significant snowfall and is reopened in late spring.

A child's walk among tundra's treasures followed by a downhill hike through a wind-sculpted forest are what makes this combination of trails a delight for children of all ages.

Easily accessible from the Mount Evans Highway, the Alpine Garden Loop starts at 12,140 feet, changing little in elevation as it loops around a rocky crest. Views of Chicago Lakes Basin dominated by 14,258-foot Mount Evans first capture everyone's interest at this windy summit. (An extra jacket, preferably hooded and windproof, is a must for this hike!)

Before embarking on the hike, allow children to explore the rocky outcrop near the parking lot. Children love to climb these boulders, discovering new vistas and windless nooks where begging chipmunks can be expected. (In state parks, feeding wild animals, even those cute chipmunks, is illegal.)

The trail begins just off the highway adjacent to the trail sign. Here, hikers enter a field of rocks called a "fellfield." Even though wind prevents snow and rain from accumulating here, tiny flowers grow among the rocks. (As they peer closely, guard your children's eyes from unnoticed sharply pointed grasses.) In early summer, hikers are likely to find Alpine forget-me-nots, a mat of tiny sky blue flowers with a yellow center. To demonstrate why flowers in this area are short, have the children feel and compare the power of wind when standing tall and when crouched low like the flowers.

Circling around the rocky summit, the Alpine Garden Loop distance meets the Mount Goliath Trail, marked by a trail post. Groups of two adults with hikers of mixed ability can separate here. While the Goliath hikers continue their 1-mile trek, the adult with the loop trail hikers continues on the loop trail and, when finished, drives to Mount Goliath Trail's end, 1.8 miles north of the alpine loop parking lot. The group reunites at the highway pulloff.

Those who walk the Mount Goliath Trail are treated to unobstructed vistas in the Mount Evans massif as they descend into a stand of bristlecone pines. Children are surprised to learn these trees are among the oldest living things on earth—1500 to 2000 years old! (The oldest bristlecone pine, found in Nevada, shows 4964 growth rings.) The relentless forces of timberline wind have twisted and gnarled bristlecone pines into bizarre, imagination-teasing shapes. Encourage your children to find faces and creatures in these artfully scoured trees. The last 0.3

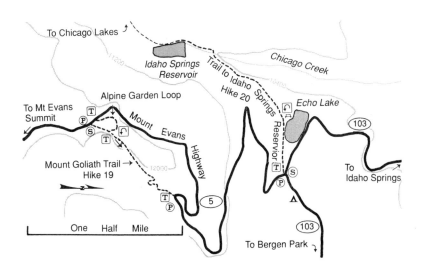

An alpine nook lures children, wildflowers, and chipmunks.

mile of trail winds through a thick stand of conically shaped bristlecone pines growing in a relatively windless area. Point out how this same variety of tree can grow full and symmetrical when not shaped by nature's forces.

Toilet and picnic facilities are available at the Echo Lake Campground.

20. Echo Lake to Idaho Springs Reservoir

Location: Arapaho National Forest
Type: Day hike or backpack
Difficulty: Moderate for children
Hikable: June–October
Distance: 1.7 miles, one way
Starting elevation: 10,640 feet
High point: 10,800 feet
Maps: Arapaho National Forest, USGS Idaho Springs

Driving Directions: See directions for hike 19, Alpine Garden Loop and Mount Goliath Trails. From the parking lot near Echo Lake where CO-103 and Mount Evans Highway (CO-5) intersect, walk up the Mount Evans Highway 50 yards to the point at which power lines cross above the road. The trailhead is in the trees directly below, on the right.

Be it a picnic lunch beside a lake, an afternoon fishing jaunt, or an alpine overnight, the Chicago Lakes Trail can be enjoyed by hikers of all sizes and interests.

Hikers begin their walk on a level path through a spruce forest. The trail passes through sparsely vegetated undergrowth where foot traffic is not evident. Ask the kids to watch for trail markers or blazes on trees. In doing so they'll notice "old man's beard," a gray-green hair-like growth hanging from tree branches. This lichen lives off dead matter on the tree but doesn't harm it. Using the lichen as hair and bits of wood for the body, kids can make a gnome doll.

Within the first 100 yards, the trail reaches the south side of Echo Lake, paralleling it for another 0.2 mile to a picnic destination for very young hikers. From here, the trail jogs a bit to the left before it enters a boulder-dotted area and veers south. Watch for views of the mountains above Chicago Lakes from this point.

Limber pines dominate the forest here. Introduce this tree to your children by having them carefully bend its young, seemingly

Young hikers on the trail

elastic branches. Also, ask them to count its needles, which grow in clumps of five.

Descending 200 feet to the reservoir, the trail zigzags via shallow switchbacks through the forest to a rushing creek below. After crossing this creek spilling from the reservoir, the trail joins an old four-wheel-drive road. Continue walking 0.7 mile slightly uphill on the road leading to Idaho Springs Reservoir. At the reservoir, those with fishing gear have a good chance of catching supper. Those with backpacks can continue their hike another 2.3 miles south to Chicago Lakes, nestled in an alpine basin at 11,600 feet.

Return via the same route.

---

21. Dunes Exploration

Location:	Great Sand Dunes National Monument
Type:	Dayhike
Difficulty:	Easy for children
Hikable:	Year-round
Distance:	0.3 to 4 miles, one way
Starting elevation:	8150 feet
High point:	8850 feet
Map:	Great Sand Dunes National Monument brochure

Driving Directions: Take US 160 east from Alamosa 26 miles to CO-150. Turn north and travel 19 miles to the park entrance and visitor center. To reach the parking lot nearest the dunes, drive 0.3 miles north of the visitor center to a turnoff on the left.

Hiking becomes a leaping, sliding, even cartwheeling and somersaulting event at Colorado's Great Sand Dunes National Monument, where 55 square miles of sand, wind-sculpted into myriad hills and valleys, invite climbing to the crest of a dune then rolling and jumping down the hill—again and again. The day's destination may be the first knoll of sand or a trek to the top of the highest hill.

Dune explorers start their hike by splashing across Medano Creek, the ankle-deep stream adjacent to the dunes parking lot. In the spring or early summer, the creek flow is about 25 yards wide, washing the sand in peculiar wave-like pulses called "bores." After children have had fun at the crossing, point out how the creek flows in rhythms like the ocean's waves. (This motion is caused by sand granules carried in the shallow current.)

No need to watch for trail signs, simply aim for a mountain of sand on which to play. Some hills are several cartwheels away; others require a morning's hike to reach. Do bring a camera; the nearby snow-capped Sangre de Cristo Mountains add a stunning background to photographs of kids cavorting on sand. (Be sure to bring a case to protect your camera from blowing and kicked sand.)

With no ocean or lake nearby, the dunes may seem misplaced, but the ingredients for making them are here—wind, sand, and time. Over centuries, the Sangre de Cristo Mountains blocked the prevailing wind carrying sand from the San Juan Mountains (to the southwest) and San Louis Valley and pocketed it at its present base. Sand-loaded snowmelt from three creeks is also deposited here.

The dunes are a tough environment, but a few plants and animals have found their niche here. Found nowhere else on earth, the Great Sand Dunes tiger beetle and giant sand treader camel cricket may leave their tiny tracks along your "trail." Youngsters can discover how insects survive life on the hot sand by feeling the temperature difference of surface sand and the layer just below.

During hot summer months, plan your dune exploration for

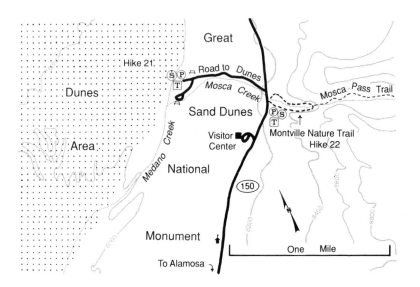

Sand Dunes exploration

the cooler hours of morning or evening. And do heed the sign warning that "Shoes should be worn at all times on the dunes." The surface temperature of the dunes can reach 140 degrees.

Toilet and picnic facilities are available near the parking lot.

22. Montville Nature Trail

Location:	Great Sand Dunes National Monument
Type:	Dayhike
Difficulty:	Easy for children
Hikable:	March–mid-November
Distance:	0.5 mile, loop
Starting elevation:	8252 feet
High point:	8362 feet
Maps:	Great Sand Dunes Montville Trail Guide, USGS Sand Dunes National Monument

Driving Directions: See directions for hike 21, Dunes Exploration. The parking lot for Montville Trail is 0.3 mile north of the visitor center on the right side of the road. The trail guide is available at the trailhead.

Paralleling both sides of Mosca Creek, this gentle trail is a cool contrast to the heat of the dunes, offering an interesting look at the forces that shape this region. Small children enjoy splashing rocks in the creek and may be rewarded with the sight of a mule deer bedded down for the day.

From the parking lot, the trail plunges into the shade of a pinyon-juniper forest with the gurgle of the creek in the background. As the trail follows the stream, it climbs gently and then descends, looping through a variety of ecosystems.

Montville Trail, named for a 30-family settlement here in the late 1800s, is part of the Mosca Pass Trail. This trail was once the only access for Indians and pioneers coming into the San Louis Valley from the east.

Mosca Creek is one of three year-round streams that drain

Aspen leaf in fall splendor

into the dunes. A variety of trees—Rocky Mountain maple, aspen, chokecherry, white fir, and Douglas fir—are supported in this moist environment, while drought-resistant plants such as yucca and rabbit brush are found in the underbrush. Along the trail ask children to count the different kinds of coniferous trees (those with *cones*) and deciduous trees (those with leaves that "decide" to change colors in fall). In doing so, they will notice dark scars across the white bark of the aspen trees. These are caused by deer eating the bark in late winter or by rubbing the "velvet" covering off their newly formed antlers in fall.

At 0.25 mile, the trail crosses the creek where it meets Mosca Pass Trail, which is a 3.5-mile climb to its 9700-foot destination in the Sangre de Cristo Mountains. Stay on the Montville Trail, and along the return side of the loop (0.4 mile) watch for the creekside rest stop, a mini-amphitheater for taking in forest sounds and smells. Panoramic views of the dunes and the adjoining San Louis Valley can also be enjoyed from this side of the trail. The trail descends via a few switchbacks that lead to a creek crossing and the trailhead.

Toilet and water facilities are available at the visitor center.

CENTRAL

(Summit County, Vail, Aspen, Crested Butte)

23. Lily Pad Lake

Location: Arapaho National Forest
Type: Dayhike
Difficulty: Moderate for children
Hikable: June–October
Distance: 2.8 miles, one way
Starting elevation: 9800 feet
High point: 10,000 feet
Maps: Dillon Ranger District,
USGS Frisco

Driving Directions: *Wildernest Trailhead.* From Silverthorne, take CO-9 (Exit 205 off I-70) north, turning west (left) at the 7-Eleven where Ryan Gulch road leads to the Wildernest Subdivision. Continue through the subdivision 2.4 miles, parking at the end of the road. The trail begins just beyond the recently constructed water tower on the hillside.

Meadow Creek Trailhead. From I-70 near Silverthorne, take Exit 203 west. Immediately north of the Information booth, turn

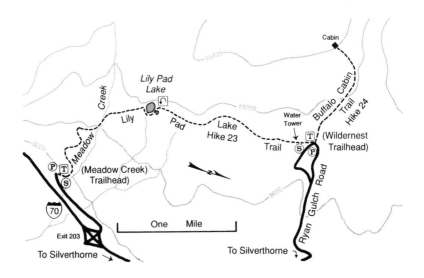

Lily Pad Lake

west onto a gravel road, continuing 0.5 mile to the trailhead parking lot.

Whether walked in its entirety with a shuttled car parked at the trail's end, or simply as a lake destination returning via the same route, the Lily Pad Lake Trail promises a delightful dayhike for every hiker. Because the lake is located in the Eagle's Nest Wilderness, bicycles are not permitted here—a refreshing change for a trail located close to an urban area.

Don't let the first 100-yard climb up the access road near Wildernest subdivision discourage little hikers. At the water tower, the trailhead enters a level lodgepole pine forest. A pleasing difference here is the array of brooks gurgling across the floor of this forest.

Typically, lodgepoles thrive in dry, well-drained soils, forming dense stands with little vegetation beneath them. However, lodgepoles are one of the first trees to reclaim a forest destroyed by fire. Examine the cone of a lodgepole pine and point out to the children how tightly closed its individual scales are. A lodgepole seed is attached to each scale. Lodgepole cones remain this way for many years until the heat of a forest fire opens them, spilling the seeds on bare ground. Can your hikers find evidence of the fire? Why or why not? Can they find lodgepole seedlings in the area?

Within 1 mile, the trail enters an aspen-pine stand where a leaking beaver pond necessitates a 25-foot-long footbridge constructed of lodgepole pine trunks. The slender trunks of these trees were used by American Indians as poles for their teepees. How does this use explain the tree's name?

Another 0.5 mile of subtle climbing leads to a lily pad–blanketed lake on the left. Adjacent to it is the larger, less flower-quilted Lily Pad Lake. The thick, heart-shaped leaf of the yellow pond lily insulates the water and its inhabitants from heat. Tell children that fishermen know the water is too deep for hipboots where "wokas," the Indian name for pond lily, grow; then ask them to point to where the water is over their heads. Remind children that it's not safe to swim in any lake in which pond lilies grow because of its depth.

 The lakes are a good destination point for a lunch stop or to head back on the same trail.

The trail follows a narrow passage between the lakes, then gradually descends for 1 mile passing through several lovely aspen stands before reaching Meadow Creek trailhead. In clearings between the trees, enjoy the views of Dillon Reservoir and the surrounding mountains. About 0.5 mile from the lakes, the trail switchbacks to a footbridge that spans Meadow Creek. (If a camera is part of your hiking gear, plan to photograph the children crossing the bridge with aspens in the background.) After the bridge, tell the hike leader to watch for the remains of a log cabin clinging to an aspen hillside on the right. Perhaps they will recognize that the structure's logs are those of a lodgepole pine. The cabin marks the trail's last 0.3 mile.

No picnic, toilet, or water facilities are available.

24. Buffalo Cabin Trail

Location:	Arapaho National Forest
Type:	Dayhike
Difficulty:	Easy to moderate for children
Hikable:	June–mid-October
Distance:	1 mile, one way
Starting elevation:	9800 feet
High point:	10,400 feet
Map:	Arapaho National Forest

Driving Directions: See directions for hike 23, Lily Pad Lake. The trail begins in the pines to the northeast.

"Little cabin in the woods" was the song I heard young hikers chant as they walked to this historic site in a lodgepole forest. They didn't find a "little ole man by the window stood," or a "rabbit hopping by," but they had fun imagining their days hiding out in the remnants of a mountain cabin.

From the parking lot near the trailhead, hikers begin a steady, though not too steep, climb through a forested hillside. Large downed lodgepoles cross the trail in numerous places. Maintenance crews have cleared the trees from the path, but you should stop to examine their exposed root systems.

Dillon Reservoir in Summit County

On hands and knees look for the remaining roots in the torn ground where the tree once stood. Young investigators will find tiny root hairs emanating from thicker root tips threading the soil, holding it in place. Compare the differences in root length and thickness. Ask which roots keep the tree upright and which transport water from the soil. If these trees were removed, what might happen to this hillside during a rainstorm? Your companions will be surprised to learn that the height of the lodgepole they're seeing aboveground can be matched in length below it. Look for evidence of insect and animal use in the downed tree.

Within 0.5 mile, the trail meets an old road. Turn left here and climb briskly to the ruins of a cabin on the right. Cross the small stream near here and walk 100 yards uphill to see a larger, roofless cabin. Little is known about the history of these log houses. There's no evidence of mining and logging activity in the area, suggesting the cabin dwellers were hunters.

Eager hikers may want to continue their climb for another 1.1 miles to the summit of Buffalo Mountain. This is not a marked route. Views of Dillon Reservoir and Blue River Valley Trail are splendid along this hike.

No picnic, toilet, or water facilities are available.

25. Surprise Trail

Location:	Arapaho National Forest
Type:	Dayhike
Difficulty:	Moderate for children
Hikable:	June–October
Distance:	2.6 miles, one way
Starting elevation:	8600 feet
High point:	10,000 feet
Maps:	Arapaho National Forest, USGS Mount Powell

Driving Directions: From Silverthorne, take CO-9 (Exit 205 off I-70) 17.6 miles north. At Heeney Road, turn left and continue 5.7 miles to County Road 1725 (Cataract Creek Road). Turn left and drive 2.4 miles to the parking lot for Surprise Trail.

Aspens are no surprise along this trail.

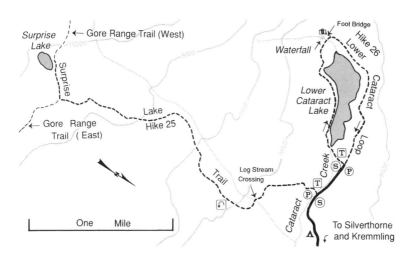

This pleasant trail follows a staircase pattern, climbing then leveling off in forests of aspen, lodgepole, and spruce and ending at Surprise Lake. Meadows, beautifully peppered with wildflowers, make a colorful destination for little hikers eager to walk 1 mile only.

The wooden footbridge directly south of the parking lot marks the trail's beginning. From here, hikers enter the Eagle's Nest Wilderness Area, gradually ascending a stand of mature aspen trees followed by a lodgepole pine forest. At 0.7 mile, youngsters crossing the creek just beyond may need a helping hand stepping on the logs that serve as a bridge.

 Throughout the summer, flowers blanket the meadow at 1 mile in a cornucopia of color. Purple lupines and lavender asters

Surprise Lake

complement the variety of yellow daisy-like flowers blooming in July and August. Towering over your shortest hiker is false hellebore. Its large pleated leaves protrude from stalks 3 to 6 feet in height topped by a branched cluster of yellow-green flowers. Youngsters enjoy playing hide and seek in these tall stands of plant life. "Big kids" are interested in learning how American Indians once used the leaves of the big plant to lower blood pressure and slow the heartbeat. But don't try such a treatment—false hellebore is fatal if taken in large quantities!

Climbing another "step," the trail enters an aspen grove with a crowd of lodgepoles edging it. At 1.7 miles, the trail levels then winds through a dense pine forest. Encourage hikers to walk softly here, perhaps they'll hear the forest "ghosts"—the creaking sound of partially fallen lodgepoles being moved by the wind.

Within 0.5 mile, the trail forks. The trail to Surprise Lake is on the right, the Gore Range Trail is on the left. At the time of this writing, numerous revegetation signs barred direct access to this popular lake. However, at the creek just before the lake, turn left on the path that leads to the lake shore.

Return via the same route. Toilet and water facilities are available at Cataract Creek Campground.

26. Lower Cataract Loop

Location:	Arapaho National Forest
Type:	Dayhike
Difficulty:	Easy for children
Hikable:	June–October
Distance:	2 miles, one way
Starting elevation:	8630 feet
High point:	8660 feet
Maps:	Arapaho National Forest, USGS Mount Powell

Driving Directions: See directions for hike 25, Surprise Trail. The parking lot for Lower Cataract Loop Trail is 0.25 mile west of Surprise Trail's parking lot.

Floating aspen leaves on Lower Cataract Lake

Cataract Falls, visible from the trailhead, lures hikers around a mountain-fed lake and passes through sun-drenched meadows into the cool, dark corridors of an old-growth forest. The lake's beautiful serenity, especially in the morning, sets the tone for quiet discoveries in the brooks, brush, and shore along the trail. Weekday use of this popular walk is recommended. Camping and bicycles are not permitted within 0.25 mile of the lake or along the trail.

At the trailhead, located just west of the parking lot, take the 0.25-mile middle path, which leads directly to the lake. Just before reaching the lake's shore, turn left, crossing the footbridge spanning a creek draining from the lake. As the trail climbs a bit above the lake, it meanders past several springs percolating the rich, dark soil. Riparian zones such as these attract a wide array of wildlife. Encourage children to watch for birds and insects frequenting the area.

Don't let the numerous spur trails confuse you; most of them have been blocked by rocks or logs and lead in the direction of the falls (0.9 mile) at the lake's south end. Before reaching them, watch on the trail's right side for a four-hug-wide ponderosa pine, now standing as a snag. The dead tree provides homes and food for birds, rodents, and insects. Linger here to see how creatures use the tree. (A squirrel may scamper into a cavity in the limb. A woodpecker may alight on the trunk to drill a hole in search of insects.)

For a lunch stop, Lilliputian style, stop at the tiny, grass-covered island adjacent to the lake, just past the ponderosa snag. However, the thundering of waterfalls may draw hikers onward into the old-growth forest. Providing full view of the falls, a boardwalk bridge spans the widest section of the creek foaming below them.

Explorers eager to see more of the cascading water can scramble the steep wall of trees and rocks to the left. After a photography stop on the bridge, follow the trail to the right.

Within 25 yards of the bridge the trail edges a calm section of the creek where wading and picnicking is in order. Beyond here, the trail circles the lake's southwest edge passing through tall grass meadows then climbing slightly into an aspen glade. At 1.5 miles, the trail meets the wilderness boundary fence. Please respect the private property below the trail. Follow the trail through the spruce-aspen forest for 0.4 mile.

Before leaving the forest to meet the roadway back to the parking lot, look for ground squirrels' middens under the spruce trees on the left. Beneath the thick mat of spruce cone pieces, the rodents store their winter food. Ask the children to find the ground squirrels' entry holes into the midden.

27. Rock Creek

Location: Arapaho National Forest
Type: Dayhike or backpack
Difficulty: Moderate for children
Hikable: June–September
Distance: 1.6 miles, one way
Starting elevation: 9500 feet
High point: 10,200 feet
Maps: Arapaho National Forest,
USGS Willow Lakes

Driving Directions: From Silverthorne, follow CO-9 for 8.2 miles north to a dirt road opposite the Blue River Campground. Turn west (left) and drive 1.4 miles to a road on the left directing you to Rock Creek. Continue 1.6 miles to the parking area.

A hike through a bird nesting area to an abandoned mine surrounded by magnificent mountain vistas makes this a trip for the whole family. Access to the Eagle's Nest Wilderness in the Gore Range is another attraction of this trail.

From the parking lot, walk westerly into the forest to meet the Rock Creek trailhead. From here, the trail begins on an old road before it reaches the wilderness gate. It maintains a steady,

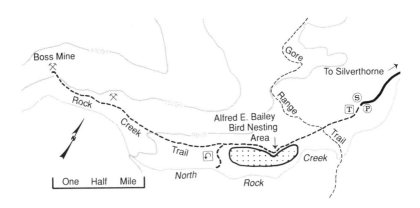

gradual route up Rock Creek valley, crossing the Gore Range trail within the first 0.5 mile. (A number of backpack destinations are available on this trail.) The Alfred E. Bailey Bird Nesting Area is entered 0.1 mile after the trail intersects the Gore Range Trail.

Alert your companions to watch for yellow-streaked birds. Pine siskins and yellow-rumped warblers, both common birds here, wear yellow. The siskin's coloring is drab compared to the vibrant gold throat, cap, rump, and flanks of the warbler. However, if a yellow-colored bird is sighted hanging upside down plucking seeds from pine cones, the acrobat is a siskin. If one of the children spies a bird in this vicinity wearing an aluminum leg band, it is one that has been tagged for a study on the species that visit and breed in this zone.

Youngsters who fail to *see* any birds are guaranteed to *hear* a musical concert given by the winged forest dwellers. Encourage the kids to notice different bird calls and try to imitate them. At 0.7 mile, the forest on the left gives way to views of a meadow dotted with beaver ponds. Stop to lift little ones high enough to see the beaver workings.

Just before the trail begins its short (0.4 mile), steep climb along a scree-covered ridge, a fork on the left leads to Rock Creek, a shorter destination (another 0.1 mile) for tired little legs.

A hiker's favorite sign

National Forest
WILDERNESS

Closed to motor vehicles, motorized equipment, hang gliders and bicycles

Area back of this sign is managed and protected under Public Law (16U.S.C. 551; 16U.S.C. 1131-1136)

Violations Punishable

Those who continue the additional 0.5 mile to Boss Mine are rewarded with superb views of the snowy Gore Range atop a lush green valley bisected by the roaring Rock Creek. Watch on the right side of the trail for the remains of Boss Mine's barracks—the old stove top, rusty bed frames, cabin logs, etc.—are fun to investigate.

Return is via the same trail. No toilet, water, or picnic facilities are available here.

28. Williams Fork Boardwalk

Location:	Routt National Forest
Type:	Dayhike
Difficulty:	Easy for children
Hikable:	Mid-June–late September
Distance:	1115 feet, one way
Starting elevation:	8500 feet
High point:	8500 feet
Map:	Routt National Forest

Wheelchair accessible

Driving Directions: From Silverthorne, take CO-9 for 13.8 miles north to Ute Pass Road and turn right. Travel 9.5 miles, passing Henderson Mill to the Sugarloaf and South Fork campgrounds

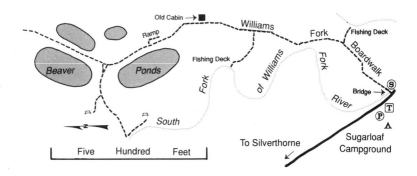

A father and son examine an oak leaf.

turnoff, County Road 30. Turn right, go 6 miles, driving through the large tunnel bridge. Turn right at the sign for South Fork Campground, continuing 0.5 mile to the beginning of Williams Fork Boardwalk on the left in Sugarloaf Campground. Handicapped parking is available for four to five cars.

Designed for individuals in a wheelchair as well as parents with young children, the Williams Fork Boardwalk provides access to a varied swath of nature in Routt National Forest. In five places, the 8-foot-wide planked boardwalk edges the Williams Fork River where fishing is reported to be great! Extensive beaver activity surrounding the elevated walkway is converting the area from pines to wet-country willows and grasses.

The boardwalk begins near the far end of Sugarloaf Campground on the left side of the roadway. The Williams Fork River meanders slowly under the boardwalk here. Encourage youngsters to look for fish resting and feeding in the pools. To show children what fish eat, have them hold a white handkerchief open then dip it across the water's surface. Insect larvae will remain on the cloth.

About halfway along the boardwalk, watch for the remnants of a log cabin. When the kids discover it (on the right) ask "How many rooms were in it? Did it have a fireplace? Electricity? Running water? Why were people living here?" (An archaeologist studying the sight believes it was a trapper's cabin.)

As the boardwalk spans the beaver pond area, near the far end, have children find brush and tree trunks stunted by the animal. Count the beaver ponds. Hoist little ones up high to see how their dams have altered the river's flow and created this wet area. Can they find pine trees that have died since water inundated the area?

Wet soils of bogs and streams support a wide variety of wildflowers. Youngsters here have fun counting flowers of different colors. Blooming at the same time as deep purple monkshood is the rarely seen pink pyrola flower. Kneeling on the boardwalk, have kids search for the little woodland plant bearing pink pearl-like flowers atop a single stem. Its heart-shaped leaves are shiny and close to the ground. Children have a knack for renaming natural things; ask yours what they want to call the flower.

Wheelchair users can make full use of the campground adjacent to the trailhead. A group campsite and five smaller campsites have been designed for wheelchair accessibility, plus the paths to the wheelchair-accessible toilet and water pump are barrier free. Two decked picnic areas adjoin the fishing ramp extensions on the boardwalk.

29. Spruce Creek

Location: Arapaho National Forest
Type: Dayhike or backpack
Difficulty: Moderate to challenging for children
Hikable: June–October
Distance: 3 miles, one way, from two-wheel-drive trailhead; 1.6 miles, one way, from four-wheel-drive trailhead
Starting elevation: 10,400 feet from two-wheel-drive trailhead; 11,080 feet from four-wheel-drive trailhead
High point: 12,200 feet
Maps: Arapaho National Forest, USGS Breckenridge

Driving Directions: From Breckenridge, on CO-9 travel 2.4 miles south turning right (east) at County Road 800 at "The Crown" subdivision. Stay on this gravel road for 1.2 miles; bear

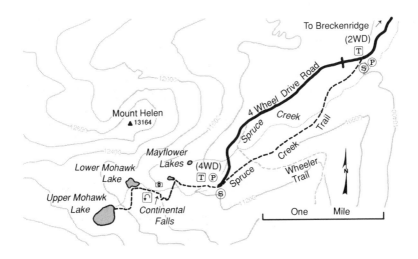

right at the first fork. Turn left at the next fork to the secon trailhead parking area on the left. Four-wheelers can continue another 1.5 miles to the next trailhead.

Cascading waterfalls and abandoned mining cabins set in an exquisite alpine cirque are what make this hike so popular. Although the trail ends after a very steep climb to Upper and Lower Mohawk lakes, 0.5 mile before the lakes is an easier, very worthwhile destination: Continental Falls spilling from a wildflower-blanketed hillside scattered with the rusty remnants of a bygone mining era. Most hikers can enjoy these sights as a dayhike—before the afternoon thunderstorms.

From the parking lot, the trail winds through an aspen wooded area for 0.5 mile before it crosses Spruce Creek via a two-log bridge. Mosquito repellant is a must for the next 0.8-mile walk through an old growth spruce forest. While passing under the stately trees, show children where woodpeckers in search of insects have drilled holes in the trunks.

Children are intrigued to learn that the tree-climbing bird removes an insect by spearing it with its long, flexible tongue. Woodpeckers also declare boundaries by dimpling dead trees.

At 1.3 miles, you meet the Wheeler trail, which leads to the Gore Range. Continue walking west to the four-wheel-drive access road. Beyond here, the trail climbs in earnest. However, as the trees thin, glimpses of waterfalls lure young hikers 0.2 mile uphill. At the crest of the climb, a good place to catch your breath is at the mining cabins (some of which can be entered). Remind youngsters to respect the delicate nature of these and other historic structures. To view the Continental Falls, follow the trail 0.2 mile northwest. The big, bald peak to the north of the mined area is 13,164-foot Mount Helen.

Eager hikers like to scramble the very steep 0.5-mile path alongside and above the falls to Lower Mohawk Lake. In doing so, they pass the top station of an old mining tramway. Notice the cart's big bull wheel and wooden brakes. Another 0.5 mile farther is Upper Mohawk Lake, surrounded by showy, scree-laden mountains. Backpackers intending to camp at the lakes should remember to camp at least 100 feet from the water.

Return is via the same trail or the four-wheel-drive road. No toilet, water, or picnic facilities are available at either site.

The bull wheel near Continental Falls

30. Mount Sherman

Location: Pike National Forest
Type: Dayhike
Difficulty: Challenging for children
Hikable: July–September
Distance: 2 miles, one way
Starting elevation: 11,800 feet
High point: 14,036 feet
Maps: Pike National Forest, USGS
Mount Sherman

Driving Directions: From Fairplay, travel 1.2 miles south on US 285 to Four Mile Creek Road (Forest Service Road No. 421). Turn west (right) and continue approximately 12 miles until the road is no longer accessible for two-wheel-drive vehicles. Limited parking is available alongside the road.

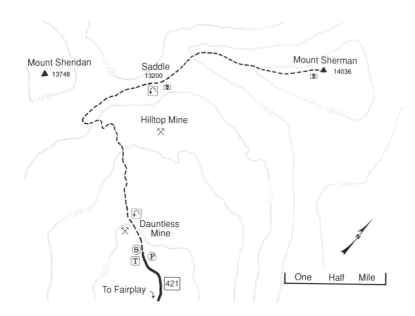

Looking north from Mount Sherman summit

Climbing a "fourteener" is perhaps the ultimate goal of most hikers in Colorado. And because nearly all of the state's 54 mountains higher than 14,000 feet challenge even experienced hikers, children often miss out on this experience. However, the climb up Mount Sherman, at 14,036 feet, is made for healthy, prepared kids.

Preparation begins with being well rested and properly equipped. Nothing fancier than sturdy hiking shoes, rain gear, a warm sweater, a hat, sunscreen, high-energy food, and at least one quart of water per person is required. Preparation also means starting the hike very early in the morning and watching for weather changes. Warn your companions that they'll have to head back should clouds start blanketing the sky; weather changes can be sudden and severe above the tree line.

Mount Sherman is visible from the road where most two-wheel-drive cars park. No trailhead marks the route up the peak; simply continue following the rocky, four-wheel-drive road. Within 0.5 mile, you will reach the buildings of the Dauntless Mine. Do not enter the mine because it is rather dilapidated. Before leaving the area, point out the support timbers called "deadmen" on the left between the two buildings, which reinforce the loose rock around the mine entrance. Near the mine entrance is the small rail line and its ore carts.

Bear right after the last building of the Dauntless Mine. Notice the spongy soil supporting tiny alpine flowers. Beyond here it's rocks only to the summit. At about 0.8 mile, bear left toward a small log structure then continue around it to the right. The trail becomes more visible as it approaches the saddle below Mount Sherman. Have youngsters look for "cairns" or piles of rocks marking the route. The buildings to the right, about 0.2 mile below the saddle (a pass between peaks), are from the Hilltop Mine.

At 1.5 mile, you'll come upon the saddle, which is at 13,200 feet and is a good place to rest (if necessary, turn back). To the west is Leadville; to the east South Park and Pikes Peak. Notice the snow accumulation on the leeward side of the ridge. Explain that these "cornices" build up as the wind blows from the windward side. Cornices sometimes break off in spring causing an avalanche. Also notice the electric lines crossing the saddle. Power from Leadville is supplied to Fairplay through these lines.

The last 800-foot ascent to the summit is slow going. Look for cairns that basically head straight up the ridge of Mount Sherman. At one point, for nearly 75 yards, the trail is only 4 to 6 feet wide with steep dropoffs on both sides. Take extra care here. As the trail nears the peak, the grade eases and you pass a "false summit." Continue walking approximately 0.1 mile north to reach the real summit of Mount Sherman. The views are good in all directions. The Collegiate Range is to the west past Leadville. Mount Massive and Mount Elbert, the state's two highest peaks, are visible.

Kids are surprised to find plant and animal life at 14,000 feet. Marmots and pikas whistle from the rocks, and small birds get moisture from the old snow fields. Tiny flowers blossom beneath the rocks all the way up to the summit.

Before descending, have kids look to the east to spot their car. It may just be a speck of light reflected from the sun.

Consider this hike "open" after July 1. Before that time, snow fields may block the route.

31. Wagon Wheel Loop No. 1429-1427

Location: Pike and San Isabel National Forests
Type: Dayhike or backpack
Difficulty: Moderate to challenging for children
Hikable: June–October
Distance: 3.8 miles, loop
Starting elevation: 8970 feet
High point: 9600 feet
Maps: Pike & San Isabel National Forest, USGS Mount Antero

Driving Directions: From Buena Vista, take US 285 south about 9 miles to County Road 270. Follow this dirt road for 1.5 miles west where it becomes County Road 272. Continue for 2 miles to an intersection. Turn left and proceed another 1.5 miles to Browns Creek Trailhead on the right.

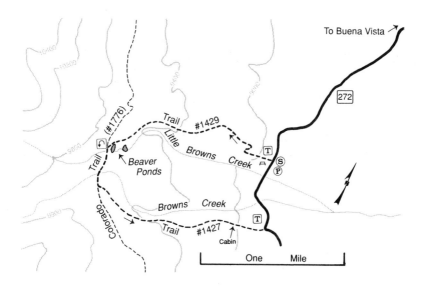

An antler-scarred aspen tree on Wagon Wheel Loop

A stunning view of a "fourteener," opportunities for trout fishing, a close look at a beaver subdivision, and an abundance of wildlife make the Wagon Wheel Loop a delightful dayhike. It can also be the beginning of an extended trip to a peak in the Collegiate Range by joining the Colorado Trail, which intersects both sides of this loop trail.

From the trail register, located on the right side of a turn-around for horse trailers, the trail switches back up a hill. This steep, but short (0.3-mile) climb rewards hikers with views of Mount Shavano (one of Colorado's 54 mountains over 14,000 feet high) to the north and, to the south, the Arkansas River Valley rimmed by the Sangre de Cristo range. A gently rolling path through a pine and aspen forest follows.

Hikers of any age notice that most of the aspen trees here are scarred with 3- to 5-inch rectangular slashes. The scars were caused by deer eating the tree bark or when the animal rubbed its antlers against it. Encourage your forest investigators to examine the scars closely. Perhaps they will find deer teeth marks embedded in a tree.

Another, more common aspen marking is the elongated black knot along the trunk. A branch once grew where the scar is. As- pen, intolerant of shade, drop their lower branches as they grow taller. The remaining scar looks surprisingly similar to a human eye. Children can have fun pretending the "aspen eye" is following them as they walk through the forest.

At 1.3 miles, a series of ponds and beaver dams borders the trail's left side. It's worth the effort to wander close to the stilled waters of Little Browns Creek and perhaps catch a glimpse of nature's construction engineers.

Those wanting trout for supper should try their skills at both Browns and Little Browns creeks, crossed within 0.3 mile of each other. Sturdy log footbridges span both of these usually raging waters. The Colorado Trail intersects both No. 1429 and No. 1427 before and after the creek crossings.

As No. 1429 heads south, it meets the Colorado Trail. Take the downhill route to the east (left). Football-sized rocks, rounded from miles of creek bed tumbling, clutter the trail; hiking shoes with ankle support are a must for this hike. Remnants of an old log cabin, notched Lincoln-log style, edge the trail at 2.5 miles.

When the trail meets Forest Service Road 272, follow it to the left about 0.4 mile to the parking lot.

Toilet and picnic facilities are available at the Browns Creek Trailhead.

32. E. Alfred Marquard Nature Area

Location: Buena Vista
Type: Dayhike
Difficulty: Easy for children
Hikable: Year-round
Distance: 0.5 mile, loop
Starting elevation: 7954 feet
High point: 7954 feet
Maps: None
Wheelchair accessible

Driving Directions: From the only stoplight on Buena Vista's Main Street, turn east and travel 2 blocks, then turn south on Railroad Avenue. Proceed 0.2 mile to the middle school parking lot. A large sign marks access to the nature area.

Involvement is what makes this wheelchair-accessible nature trail a fun environment for kids of all ages. Creek wading, peering from behind a bird blind, searching for stream insects,

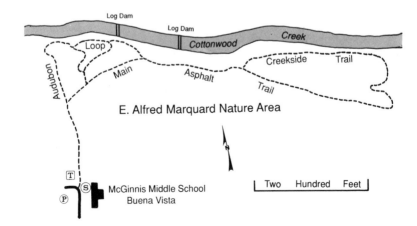

even fishing for brown trout are the kinds of learning experiences designed into the E. Alfred Marquard Nature Area.

Inspired by the potential of a neglected stream on school property, two teachers at Buena Vista's public school instigated this outdoor classroom in 1986. Their students developed the site and wrote the interpretive material for each of the eight learning stations. Several state and national awards have recognized their efforts, marking the Buena Vista nature area as a model outdoor learning center.

To reach the nature area, follow the paved walkway heading east, crossing the grassy field to the trees. Among the greenery are the trail and Cottonwood Creek, 20 feet wide and ankle deep. Log dams, placed by the students, have created deep water pools and a diversity of stream habitats here. Lush tree and plant life

One of the interpretive signs along the E. Alfred Marquard Nature Trail

borders the trail, providing shade and an abundance of wildlife zones.

Interpretive signs, written for the fifth-grade reader, provide information and questions that encourage kids to investigate on their own. For example, at the "Common Stream Insects" station, readers are told to "Pick up a rock in the stream. Inspect its surface. How many insects are on it?" The questions that follow are open-ended and involve a variety of thinking skills.

Waterfowl and other birds attracted to riparian zones can be viewed at the south end of the trail from behind the bird blind in the "Audubon Loop" spur. And those who prefer tubing or wading for summertime fun can get wet in the irrigation canal that parallels the stream. Adult supervision is required here.

Return via the shaded nature trail or the paved walkway that borders the irrigation ditch and the dry upland terrain of cacti and sage.

---

33. Missouri Lakes Trail No. 2003

Location:	White River National Forest
Type:	Dayhike
Difficulty:	Moderate to challenging for children
Hikable:	Late June–September
Distance:	3 miles, one way
Starting elevation:	10,000 feet
High point:	11,380 feet
Maps:	White River National Forest, USGS Mount of the Holy Cross, USGS Mount Jackson

Driving Directions: From Vail, take I-70 west to Minturn, exiting on US-24 (Exit 171). Head south 14 miles to Homestake Road No. 703. Turn right and continue 8.1 miles to Forest Road No. 704. Turn right. In 2.3 miles, you will see large aqueduct pipes of

Cooling hot, little feet in Cottonwood Creek

the Homestake I water project. Here the road turns sharply to the right with the roadside parking area and trailhead on the left. This trail begins in the Holy Cross Wilderness. Mountain bikes are not permitted on it. Numerous forest service campgrounds and primitive campsites are along the road to the Missouri Lakes trailhead.

Missouri Creek's alluring path of waterfalls and flower-rimmed cascades draws you to its exquisite source—an alpine basin jeweled by a dozen pristine lakes. Even tired little ones resist turning back before reaching the lakes at the top.

From the parking lot bordering the Holy Cross Wilderness, Missouri Lakes Trail starts in a deciduous-coniferous forest passing close to the remnants of a log cabin at 0.2 mile on the left. Stop to let youngsters examine how the logs were notched enabling them to be stacked.

Another sight to behold in the forest undergrowth here is crimson columbines, rare compared to the large blue-and-white state flower more commonly seen in mountain meadows and aspen groves. A hummingbird may frequent the red flower, a stop that not only provides nectar for the bird, but also results in pollination of the flower, thus making its seed. Children who understand how each species is dependent on another for propagation will leave the crimson columbine unpicked, ready to be enjoyed by the next hummingbird or hiker. (Picking blue columbines is prohibited in Colorado.)

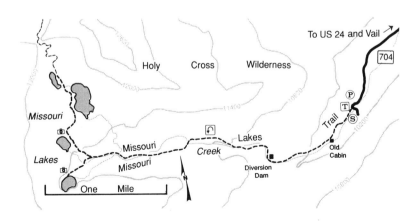

The columbine is Colorado's state flower.

Within 1 mile, the scene changes abruptly to the scars of a water development project. Pass the cement aqueducts and diversion dam above the hill to the right. (This water is being diverted and stored for residents of Colorado's Front Range cities.) Back in the forest, the creek resumes its full torrent. The trail accompanies it, climbing a steep, rocky slope.

Each time (count them!) the trail crosses Missouri Creek a footbridge spans it. Stop at these crossings to feel the cool breeze spewing from the raging creek. At 1.8 miles, just past one of these coolers, have kids look to the left, through the trees, for an unforgettable view of the creek pounding through a miniature canyon.

Meet the creek in a calm state just 0.2 mile farther. Here the creek spills into a quiet, shallow pool mirroring the surrounding

One of the Missouri Lakes in spring

peaks. A few may prefer to stay at this soothing spot while others follow the trail around the alpine marsh and into the forest. Again, the creek resumes its cascading style until it reaches the timberline 1 mile farther. Following the trail can be tricky in this wet area, but try not to wander off the path—alpine tundra is very delicate.

The lakes are a sight to behold, but this pristine destination cannot tolerate the impact of camping. Please do not build camp-fires near here.

Return is via the same trail.

34. Eagle's Nest and Gore Range Loop Trails

Location: Vail Mountain
Type: Dayhike
Difficulty: Easy for children
Hikable: Mid-May–Labor Day,
September weekends
Distance: 0.4 mile, loop, Eagle's Nest;
1.1 miles, loop, Gore Range
Starting elevation: 8156 feet
High point: 10,350 feet
Map: Vail Mountain Hiking and
Biking Trails map

Driving Directions: Access to Vail Mountain's summer hiking trail is via the Lionhead Gondola, located in the ski village office area. A fee is required for the gondola ride.

This hike provides a magnificent 360-degree view of the mountains around Vail, plus a close-up look at the plants and animals of alpine terrains. Better yet, the fourteen-minute gondola ride to the Eagle's Nest trailhead makes the experience fun and effortless.

A sweater and rain gear are recommended for this timberline destination where weather changes are swift and unsuspected. Fair-skinned folks should bring sunscreen; sun exposure at this

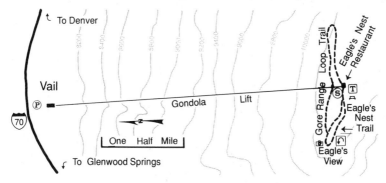

altitude is 40 percent greater than it is at sea level. Afternoon showers are common here, so plan your walk for the morning hours.

Once out of the gondola, children automatically scamper to the ridgetop straight ahead. The trail starts here but do stop to find the mythical cross of snow spread across the face of the Holy Cross Range. For some, the cross is difficult to discern because the right arm was destroyed in a rock slide. But a keen-eyed young hiker advised me to look at the biggest mountain in the group where the cross is at an angle to the lift. A photograph of the cross, taken by pioneer photographer William Henry Jackson in 1873, accompanies the interpretive sign here.

To walk the Eagle's Nest Loop, follow the trail to the right. Interpretive signs are provided to acquaint visitors with common plants and animals of the alpine zone. The Gore Range Loop joins Eagle's Nest within 0.3 mile.

Magnificent views of the Holy Cross Range to the south and the Gore Range to the west are among the attractions from this viewpoint. Skiers enjoy seeing a green version of Vail's most popular runs.

Little ones, however, may be drawn to such smaller spectacles as tiny wildflowers peeking between rocks or a patch of winter's snow lingering in the shade of a boulder. The high-pitched whistle of a pika or whistle pig (also known as rock rabbit and coney) may lure youngsters across the meadow in futile pursuit. More often heard than seen, the rabbit-like creature collects and dries grasses in miniature haystacks, hence its name "haymaker." If a storm approaches, the pika moves the food under a rock. By summer's end he can boast almost 50 pounds of greenery to live on during the winter. Watch for the pika's bundles drying on a rock in the sun.

As the trail passes around the ridgetop's only stand of trees, at 0.2 mile, it meets the 1.1-mile Gore Range Loop on the right. Those intending to explore more alpine terrain while staying on an even grade should follow this trail to the north. The Eagle's Nest Loop returns to the gondola, as does the Gore Range Loop.

The gondola at Vail Mountain

35. Hanging Lake Trail

Location:	White River National Forest
Type:	Dayhike
Difficulty:	Challenging for children
Hikable:	Year-round
Distance:	1.2 miles, one way
Starting elevation:	6110 feet
High point:	7160 feet
Maps:	White River National Forest, USGS Shoshone

Driving Directions: Travel 22 miles west of Eagle on I-70. The Hanging Lake parking area is on the right in the middle of Glenwood Canyon, at the time of this writing a highway construction site.

Unforgettably beautiful and located just off I-70, it is little wonder that Hanging Lake is one of Colorado's most popular hiking destinations. The trail climbs 1000 feet along a geologic fault line to reach the turquoise lake and waterfalls. Frequent rest stops (benches are provided) to examine the changing terrain make the hike less strenuous.

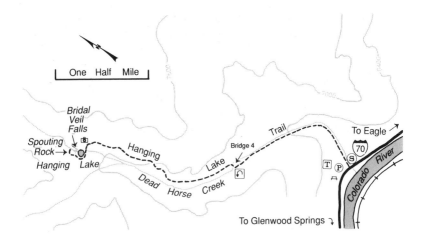

Bridal Veil Falls near Hanging Lake

The fragile environment here coupled with heavy use of the area means hikers should take extra care to leave not a trace. During summer months, avoid the crowds and heat by planning to hike in the early morning or late afternoon.

From the parking lot, the trail steadily climbs Dead Horse Canyon, crossing Dead Horse Creek several times. During spring and summer the creek runs full; however, later in the season portions of it flow underground. Have kids count each time a foot-bridge spans the creek bed.

 The light-colored stone high above bridge 2 at 0.2 mile is considered fossiliferous, but you can get a close-up look at prehistoric plant and animal life merely by examining the fossil-scarred rock in the middle of the trail.

While resting at bridge 4 (at 0.6 mile, you're halfway there!), kids will enjoy searching for Smoky Bear's cave in the rock wall, about 200 feet up. A small log cabin shelter sits on the trail's left side just 20 yards beyond.

The steepest leg of the trip begins at bridge 5 (0.7 mile). Take it slow enough to point out the old horse stables near bridge 6 (0.8 mile). In 1910 visitors at Hanging Lake Resort, located near the Colorado River, rode horses up this canyon trail.

Metal pipe guardrails add a measure of safety to the final staircase-like pathway leading to Hanging Lake. Still, youngsters will need a helping hand.

At the top of the climb, follow the boardwalk to the right circling around Hanging Lake. A geologic fault caused the lake bed to drop away from the valley floor above, hence its name. You'll want to stop and feast your eyes on Bridal Veil Falls spilling into the lake's crystal blue waters. Children, however, like to run ahead to climb on the boulders near the waterfall. (Bring a camera on this hike.) Remind youngsters to stay on the path: the shoreline is fragile. It is composed of dissolved carbonates, deposited as the water flows over the edge.

To see Spouting Rock and the lake below it, double back over the boardwalk, turn right, and walk 0.2 mile. The spout of water gushing from a hole in the center of a rock wall is caused by an underground stream finding a hole in the cliff.

In midsummer butterflies of many colors and sizes alight on the shore, seemingly teasing children to run and catch them.

Return is via the same trail. Public restrooms and a drinking fountain are maintained during the summer months. The area is closed to fishing, swimming, and camping.

36. Maroon Lake and Crater Lake Trail

Location:	White River National Forest
Type:	Dayhike
Difficulty:	Moderate for children
Hikable:	June–September
Distance:	1.75 miles, one way, Crater Lake Trail; 1.25 miles, loop, Maroon Lake Scenic Trail
Starting elevation:	9580 feet
High point:	10,076 feet
Maps:	White River National Forest, USGS Maroon Bells

Wheelchair accessible for 250 yards

Driving Directions: Take CO-82 in Aspen 0.5 mile west to Maroon Creek Road. Drive 0.5 mile to the parking lot for Aspen Highlands to meet the Roaring Fork Transit Authority bus (and pay a fee) that leaves for Maroon Lake Campground.

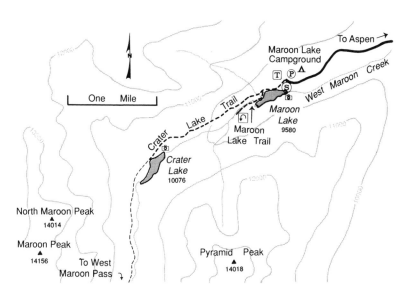

The Maroon Bells, Colorado's most photographed peaks, are a destination few visitors to the area can resist. The popular mountains are visible from the trailhead at Maroon Lake, but the sight of a splashing creek and shoulder-high flowers lure children to Crater Lake where the mountain and lake scene is majestic. Families with toddlers may prefer seeing the "Bells" from the Maroon Lake Scenic Trail, which circles the lake. A camera is a must for this hike.

Popularity, however, breeds restrictions. To reduce the impact of automobile traffic on the area (Snowmass Wilderness), during summer months the access road, Maroon Creek Road, is closed to vehicle traffic from 8:30 A.M. to 5:00 P.M. daily. Families wishing to see Maroon Bells must take Aspen's RFTA bus, which leaves Aspen Highlands parking lot every half hour. The informative ride to the trailhead at Maroon Lake Campground takes 20 minutes.

Two trails are visible from the trailhead at Maroon Lake: the Maroon Lake Scenic Trail, which loops around the lake and to the right of it, and the Maroon Bells–Snowmass Trail (also called Crater Lake Trail No. 1975), which leads to Crater Lake. Those in wheelchairs can access the trail from a two-car handicapped parking lot at Maroon Lake's north outlet. The trail is initially paved (100 yards) followed by a naturally hardened path that extends another 150 yards to a midpoint alongside the lake.

Hikers to Crater Lake initially meander through a meadow where 2- to 5-foot-tall green gentian plants (sometimes called "miner's candle") seem to light the way. Columbines, competing for attention, grow in profusion after the first bridge crossing at less than 0.5 mile. Warning: nature has devised its own defense against trampling the flowers—nettles. Children cry when they accidentally discover the plant, but if you carefully coax them into inspecting the cause of their pain, they may know what to avoid next time they walk in a field. Watch for an innocent-looking green plant with narrow, serrated leaves well armed with stinging, barely visible spines.

Beyond the meadow, the trail climbs for the remaining mile into a mixed forest. At the top of a short, steep hill a sign for the Maroon Bells–Snowmass Trail is accompanied by another one warning of sudden weather changes and steep terrain. Heavy use by inexperienced hikers on this trail has prompted the Forest Service to post this sign. Please respect the warning.

The Maroon Bells

The trail levels off just before reaching Crater Lake. The Maroon Bells, looming proud and snow-dusted, form a perfect backdrop for photos and lunch. Chipmunks will beg you to spare a crust or two for them, but don't relent. Feeding wild animals, even cute chipmunks, is illegal and also interferes with their natural food-gathering skills.

Before leaving this postcard-perfect spot, check to make sure not a trace, not a peanut shell, remains. Return is via the same trail.

Toilet and water facilities are available at the Maroon Lake campground.

37. Hallam Lake Loop Walk

Location:	Aspen Center for Environmental Studies
Type:	Dayhike
Difficulty:	Easy for children
Hikable:	Year-round
Distance:	0.4 mile, loop
Starting elevation:	7970 feet
High point:	7970 feet
Maps:	None

Wheelchair accessible (portions of)

Driving Directions: Aspen Center for Environmental Studies is located at 100 Puppy Smith Street, one block west of the U.S. Post Office. A donation is requested.

Visitors to the Aspen Center for Environmental Studies (ACES), located in the heart of Aspen, get a close-up look at how wild and orphaned animals adjust to life in a natural setting. This wildlife sanctuary is a place where children who walk quietly or stand silently are rewarded with sightings of a trumpeter swan,

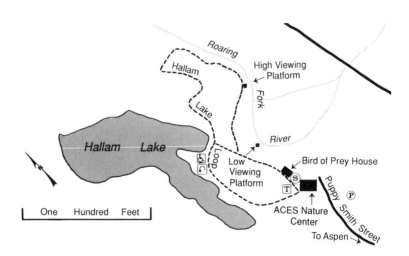

Eye to eye with a golden eagle at Hallam Lake

or a beaver, or any number of permanent wildlife residents at this 22-acre preserve. In the summer, plan this outing for the morning "Bird of Prey" hour (11:00 A.M.) when the resident golden eagle is walked while its trainer describes how the animal is cared for. Guided snowshoe walks are offered during the winter.

Access to the trail is via the cottonwood-shaded lane just outside the ACES nature center. Before starting the hike, stop here to scan the nature displays or learn about regularly scheduled naturalist walks here and in the Aspen area. A Hallam Lake Trail guide may be borrowed at the center.

A wheelchair-accessible boardwalk takes hikers approximately 30 yards from the nature center across a marshy area and alongside a lake and several beaver ponds. Here, children enjoy using binoculars (available at the nature center) to scan the waters in search of beavers or swans. Canadian geese are likely to honk their annoyance at your presence. Wheelchair use is not recommended beyond here, but the path to the Bird of Prey House behind here is suitable for wheelchair use.

he trail guide for interesting interpretations of the
on this trail winds through. Take time to scale the
form, located at signpost 23, on the left side of the
here children have a bird's-eye view of a riparian
ırage them to keep their eyes open for jays, magpies,
red-wᵢₙ₉ ₗ blackbirds, woodpeckers, or even a great blue heron
fishing in the Roaring Fork River below.

The last portion of the loop passes the Bird of Prey House
where injured or orphaned birds are housed and maintained.
Hawks and great horned owls are among the recovered residents
here. Remind children that these animals are now accustomed to
human presence and their behavior is not typical of animals in
the wild.

The Hallam Lake Trail guide and binoculars should be returned to the nature center.

38. The Grottos

Location: Aspen
Type: Dayhike
Difficulty: Easy for children
Hikable: June–October
Distance: 0.8 mile, loop
Starting elevation: 10,000 feet
High point: 10,020 feet
Map: USGS New York
Wheelchair accessible

Driving Directions: From CO-82 in Aspen, travel 10.2 miles
south to a Forest Service campground sign on the right. Continue
0.9 mile farther, just beyond the 25 mph sign, and turn right on
the gravel roadway.

The Roaring Fork River takes a playful route just 10 miles
south of Aspen. At The Grottos, it pools and spills over smoothly
 sculpted boulders forming quiet wading waters and a beach for
sand castle building. Adult supervision is required at all times

Fun in the sun at The Grottos

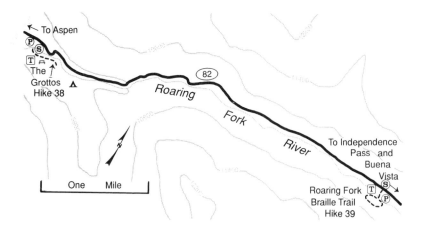

here as there are no guardrails to prevent falls into the cavernous boulders or the roaring river.

From the parking lot, the trail begins on the opposite side of the footbridge spanning the Roaring Fork. Turn left on the road-like pathway through the trees. The wheelchair sign at this intersection marks the 0.2 mile of unpaved, but smoothed and level trail leading to a set of picnic tables in the pines. Here, a portion of the river forms a shallow wading pool beside a sandy beach. Boulders piled on the shore make this a playground few children want to leave.

Those who continue on the foot trail climb a slight hill to a set of cairns on the left. Follow the footbridge over the hollowed boulders. Point out the ice formations inside the rocks. Why hasn't the ice melted? There are a few places here where children can reach into the hollows to feel the cool temperature inside them. Do not encourage anyone to climb inside the caverns.

Continue walking in the direction of the river's roar. The trail is not well marked over the smoothed granite surface, but in less than 0.2 mile it reaches the raging river and boulder display called the "Devil's Punchbowl." Hold little ones' hands as you approach the site.

Careful climbing along and back down the boulder-stacked shore leads to the picnic and beach area. Follow the wheelchair trail back to the main trail.

Toilet facilities, but no water, are available at the parking area.

39. Roaring Fork Braille Trail

Location:	Aspen
Type:	Dayhike
Difficulty:	Easy for children
Hikable:	June–October
Distance:	0.25 mile, loop
Starting elevation:	10,400 feet
High point:	10,400 feet
Maps:	None

Driving Directions: From Aspen, travel 13 miles south on CO-82. Watch for the green sign: Braille Trail 1000'. Turn right at the gravel road.

Visually impaired and sighted hikers gain a multisensory appreciation of nature on this 0.25-mile self-guided trail. A guide wire connects the trail's twenty-two interpretive stations, which

Miner's candle near Judd Falls

include sensory experiences in a spruce-fir forest, a glacial moraine, and the edge of the Roaring Fork River. Sighted children have fun wearing a blindfold on this hike.

A trail brochure is available at the trailhead sign but is not necessary because the same text is available at each station and is written in Braille and English. This trail was developed in 1967 and was the first of its kind in the world. Currently, more than 60 similar trails exist nationwide.

The trail begins in the forest adjacent to the parking lot. Before blindfolding your sighted children, allow them to experience the trail with eyes open. Remind them to not only look, but touch, smell, and listen along the way.

To accompany the blindfolded hiker, assign a partner to read the signs at each station. These messages describe ways to "see" using the other senses. Encourage hikers to let their feet be sensors; go barefoot. (During the walk make certain there are no sharp obstacles in the path.) In this way they can "see" the velvety moss or the crunchy river gravel. Listening takes on a new dimension when you ask children to listen to the direction from which the wind is rustling the willows, or in what direction the woodpecker is tapping. Find natural items for hikers to smell such as spruce needles, a rotting log, a mushroom.

After the hike share the experience by asking the following: Which sense helped the most? How could you tell if something was pretty without seeing it? Did you lose your balance? Did you hear any new sounds? How did the forest smell? Can blind people enjoy the forest as much as you?

No toilet or water facilities are available here. Free use of self-guided tapes and headphones is available at the Aspen District Forest Service office, 806 West Hallam Street, Aspen.

A family of poisonous mushrooms (Amanita muscaria)

40. Pine Creek to Morrow Point Lake

Location:	Curecanti National Recreation Area
Type:	Dayhike
Difficulty:	Moderate for children
Hikable:	June–October
Distance:	1 mile, one way
Starting elevation:	7160 feet
High point:	7340 feet
Map:	Curecanti National Recreation Area

Driving Directions: Access to the Pine Creek Trail is off US-50, 40 miles east of Montrose, or 27 miles west of Gunnison. Turn north at the sign for Pine Creek Fishing Access and Boat Tours. Drive 0.75 mile to the parking lot. Reservations for the boat tours (generally two scheduled daily, fee required) are advised, though not required. Call the Elk Creek Marina, 303-641-0707, for reservations.

A staircase descent down Black Canyon provides the only access to Morrow Point Lake, where the "Scenic Line of the World" once toured. Along the path, interpretive signs tell the story of the historic narrow-gauge railroad. A ride on the tour boat gives kids a fun lesson on the rich natural and cultural history of the

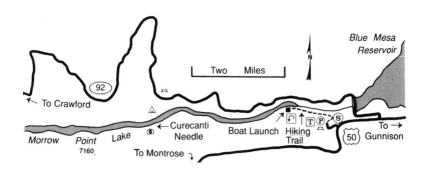

Photographing the scenery from the boat ride at Morrow Lake

area. Fishing is superb here; the water is a cold 38 degrees and fish are big.

From the parking lot, take the stairs (count them!) that descend 180 feet to Morrow Point Lake. From here the 0.75-mile trail follows the old railroad bed to the boat launch. Take time to pick the July-ripe raspberries (which tend to grow in disturbed, sun-soaked drainages) along the path. Picnic tables are also available along the trail.

The Gunnison River appears smooth and docile as you approach the launch at the end of the 0.75-mile walk. However, strong currents rage under this facade and the water level changes frequently during the day. Children should be closely supervised when near the water's edge.

Beyond the launch, the 53-mile-long Black Canyon begins 12 miles of the most awesome portion of the gorge, the narrowest, steepest, and deepest canyon in North America. During the 1.5-

Curecanti Needle

hour boat tour, the interpreter provides a lively description of the canyon's geology, history, and plant life. Wildlife sightings are frequent and become a part of the tour narrative. While on the boat you get a lake-level look at Curecanti Needle and the canyon's dark lichen-coated walls. This national recreation area is named for the Ute word for sharp point, "curecanti."

Railroad buffs interested in learning and seeing more of the passenger train that once chugged through this canyon can see its engine at the Cimmarron Information Center, approximately 25 miles east on CO-50.

Water and toilet facilities are available at the parking lot.

41. Judd Falls

Location:	Gunnison National Forest
Type:	Dayhike or backpack
Difficulty:	Easy to moderate for children
Hikable:	June–October
Distance:	0.5 mile, one way; or 1 to 5 miles, one way
Starting elevation:	9700 feet
High point:	9800 feet at Judd Falls; 11,321 feet at Copper Lake
Maps:	Gunnison National Forest, USGS Gothic

Driving Directions: Before entering the town of Crested Butte, continue northeast on CO-135 past the Mount Crested Butte Ski Area, 8 miles up Gothic Road. At the Rocky Mountain Biological Laboratory's General Store, travel 0.5 mile farther and turn right on the road. Go 0.5 mile to the Judd Falls parking lot. The trailhead is at the lot's east end.

The reward comes easy and early in this short walk through an aspen forest. The sight of Copper Creek crashing through a dark and twisted rocky chasm delights hikers of all ages. Along the way, dayhikers and backpackers en route to the Elk Mountains can't resist stopping to examine the wildflowers that splash the terrain with color.

The trail to Judd Falls stays in a friendly, flower-studded forest accompanied by a quietly babbling brook. This constant moisture enables such towering beauties as cow parsnip, a leafy stout plant topped by an umbrella of tiny white flowers, to thrive. Elk eat the succulent stem of this member of the parsley family and, although Indians and Eskimos used the plant's young shoots as food, children should not sample it. Show children the "hairs" from the plant stem. These can cause blisters around the mouth.

Also shading the trail is another tall plant, especially attractive to elk and deer, called the "monument plant." Its cone-shaped column of green-white flowers lures summer visitors of all sizes. Your children may remember the plant by its other name, "deer's ears," when you show them its leaves, shaped just like the animal's ears.

Look to the trail's right where aspen branches frame grand views of Gothic Peak cradled in the very lush East River Valley. Observant hikers will remember seeing this valley during the drive from Crested Butte to Gothic.

After the trail descends 0.1 mile on an unforested hill, turn right on the no-longer-in-use Copper Creek four-wheel-drive road. The Judd Falls overlook is only 40 feet from here on the left.

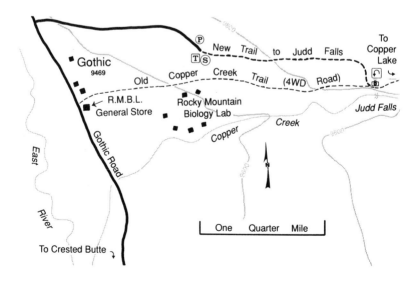

Father and son on the trail to Judd Falls

Eager amblers will need careful watching at this overlook; there are no guardrails along this 100-foot dropoff.

Return via the same trail.

Backpackers continue their hike from here following the Copper Creek Trail. This popular trek gradually ascends the creek valley with a number of beautiful meadow destinations along the way. Copper Lake, at 11,321 feet, sits at the tree line, just east of East Maroon Pass, 5 miles from the trailhead for Judd Falls.

NORTH

(Fort Collins, Rocky Mountain National Park, Steamboat Springs)

42. Pawnee Buttes

Location:	Pawnee National Grassland
Type:	Dayhike or overnight camp
Difficulty:	Easy to moderate for children
Hikable:	Year-round
Distance:	1.5 miles, one way, to the western butte; 2 miles, one way, to the eastern butte
Starting elevation:	5420 feet
High point:	5420 feet
Map:	Pawnee National Grassland

Driving Directions: From Fort Collins head east on CO-14 to Briggsdale, turning left (north) on County Road 103. Drive 4 miles, turn left on County Road 98; drive 0.75 mile to Keota. Follow County Road 105 for 2.5 miles out of Keota; turn right on County Road 104. Drive 3 miles to County Road 111, turn left. Continue driving north 4.5 miles until the road takes a sharp bend to the west. Follow the short, steep road up and around to the top of the hill where a windmill marks the parking area just north of it.

Pawnee National Grasslands is the prairie gem of northeastern Colorado. The trail leading to the two wind-scoured buttes crosses fields and gullies with limitless views in all directions.

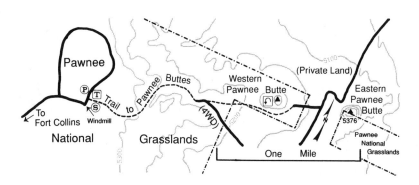

Western Pawnee Butte

For children, this nationally known study area for birds of prey is a wildlife wonderland to explore. A night spent under this giant canopy of stars, with a breeze rustling the grasses, will long be remembered.

The Pawnee Buttes are visible to the northeast from the parking area near the windmill. Follow the trail 0.2 mile down the small draw and across the field. You may encounter cows grazing in this area, which is surrounded by private land. Please respect landowners' rights. From here cross a gully and pass through a gate at 0.5 mile before reaching a saddle separating two bluffs.

The presence of yucca here indicates the presence of the yucca moth, without which the yucca could not exist. During July nights, the female moth lays her eggs in the yucca flower. In doing so she fertilizes the flower and yucca seeds are formed. As the seeds ripen, the moth larvae feed on them, leaving enough for the plant to reseed, year after year. North American Indians relied on yucca extensively. Its flower and fruit were an important food, while yucca roots were crushed to make soap, and its leaves made brooms, sandals, and rope. Ask children to feel the sharp-bladed leaves, and describe how they would use the plant.

At 0.7 mile, the trail descends into a badlands area, which is simply hills that have eroded over a long period of time. Ask children to point out other examples of badlands. From here the trail dips into a gully twice before it meets a grassland near a bluff. The western-most of the two Pawnee Buttes is visible from here.

Continue on the trail toward the buttes until you meet a jeep road at 1 mile. Follow the road for a short distance (0.1 mile) until the trail leading to the buttes reappears on the left. The trail is less obvious as it nears the buttes, but watch for the trail posts on the western butte's south side. Here the trail once again meets a jeep road, which leads to the eastern butte.

One or both buttes may be a destination for some hikers, however, climbing them is not recommended due to their crumbly clay and sandstone composition. Also, prairie falcons nesting in the area are particularly sensitive to intruders. Children can have more fun by using binoculars to watch the bird circle over its prey, then swoop down to feed.

 Exploring children need to be warned that rattlesnakes are fond of gullies and rock outcrops.

No facilities are provided for camping. Bring plenty of water and, if overnight use is planned, a cookstove.

43. Poudre River Trail

Location: Fort Collins
Type: Dayhike
Difficulty: Easy for children
Hikable: Year-round
Distance: Up to 7 miles, one way
Starting elevation: 4984 feet
High point: 4984 feet
Map: Tour De Fort bicycle map
Wheelchair accessible

Driving Directions: Foot access to the trail is via any of the streets mentioned below. Parking is available at the following locations: Taft Hill Road, north of Vine Drive; west of College Avenue, off Cherry Street; the west side of Lemay Avenue, north of Mulberry Street (also called CO-14); Seven Lakes Business Park on East Prospect; and at Northern Colorado University's Environmental Learning Center on East Drake. A Tour De Fort bicycle map is available from Fort Collins Parks & Recreation, 281 North College, in Fort Collins; phone 303-221-6640.

This wide, level, paved trail along the Cache la Poudre River is well suited for anyone who enjoys the outdoors—from children and grandparents to joggers and folks in wheelchairs. Environments vary along the trail, which is accessible in several locations throughout the year.

Located near the northern city limit of Fort Collins, the Poudre River Trail begins at Taft Hill Road and heads southeast ending at Northern Colorado University's Environmental Learning Center (open to the public) near East Drake Road.

Beginning with the trail's first mile, Taft Hill Road to Shields Street, grand views of the foothills to the west are framed by branches of cottonwood and Russian olive. During July and August, cottonwood seeds, aloft on downy feathers, drift through the air like summer's snowflakes. Encourage youngsters to gather the soft piles of seeds collected around clumps of grass and feel the softness against their faces. This section is also perfect for fall color walks. The trail continues via an underpass at Shields Street.

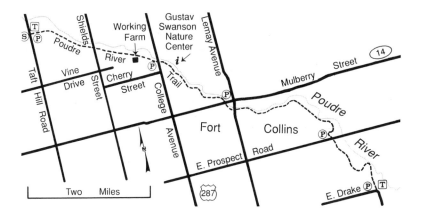

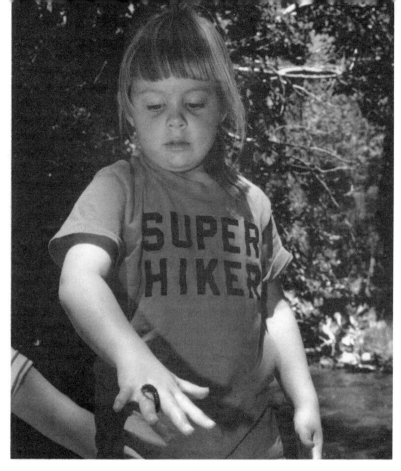

Super Hiker discovers pond life on the Poudre River Trail.

The Shields Street to College Avenue section (1.4 miles) includes a working farm at Lee Martinez Park, once the site of a dairy farm. Cows, chickens, pigs, and ponies are kept at the original barn, and the museum here contains many old farm implements. Kids will enjoy climbing the fort-like jungle gym here, while energetic folks follow the mile-long Wells Fargo Physical Fitness Trail. Others may relax on the benches along this most popular portion of the trail.

Access to the next section requires that you cross College Avenue, Fort Collins's main street, before entering the Gustav Swanson Nature Area near Linden Street. Huge narrow-leaf cottonwoods shade this 0.5-mile interpreted loop with a number of bird-viewing benches situated under the leafy canopy.

The next 0.75-mile section to Lemay Avenue is less used but meanders through lush river bed vegetation.

Access to the next section is along Lemay Avenue, across the overpass, and back down to the river. From here to East Prospect Street, this 2.75-mile interpreted trail winds through open fields, under cottonwoods, and beside ponds frequented by herons, ducks, and muskrats. Before approaching the ponds, tell children to watch for the resident black-crowned night heron. During midday he is often seen sleeping perched on a stump in the middle of the lake.

The remaining 1.2-mile portion of the trail winds between ponds and the river, ending at Northern Colorado University's Environmental Learning Center.

---

44. Kreutzer Nature Trail and Mount McConnel Summit

Location:	Roosevelt National Forest
Type:	Dayhike
Difficulty:	Moderate to challenging for children
Hikable:	May–November
Distance:	2 miles, loop, to Kreutzer Trail; additional 2.5 miles to Mount McConnel summit
Starting elevation:	6720 feet
High point:	7520 feet on Kreutzer Trail; 8000 feet at McConnel summit
Map:	Roosevelt National Forest

Driving Directions: From Fort Collins, drive 26 miles west on CO-14 to Mountain Park Campground. Turn south into the campground and continue 0.2 mile to the trailhead parking lot on the left.

Learn about the diverse forces that shape and lace the Poudre Canyon on this interpreted loop trail. Families with youngsters enjoy the Kreutzer Nature Trail's gentle climb through a variety of forests. Those with eager and able hikers continue on to ascend Mount McConnel where views of the Mummy Range and Rocky Mountain National Park are superb.

The Kreutzer trailhead is adjacent to the parking area, which is 0.2 mile past the Mountain Park Campground entrance. The hike begins in a lodgepole pine forest where the first of its twenty-two interpretive signs is at 0.3 mile. The view here, of the Poudre River Canyon and the mountains beyond, makes this an ideal destination for beginning little hikers and their parents.

As the trail maintains an easy grade, zigzagging up the river canyon, its interpretive signs allow for frequent and interesting breath-catching stops. Topics described at each sign range from lichen to mule deer, and from forest management practices to the Poudre Canyon's history.

Within 1 mile, the Kreutzer Trail meets the trail to Mount McConnel's summit. Those interested in completing the nature trail should follow the path to the right. Mountain climbers follow the switchbacks up through the ponderosa-fir forest, taking the right fork just 0.1 mile before reaching the wooded peak. At the top, the trail leading east to reconnect with the Kreutzer is rough and steep, a challenge for most hikers. The recommended return

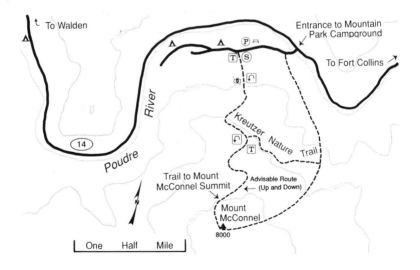

View from Mount McConnel summit

route for beginning climbers is to descend via the same route taken up.

From the Mount McConnel Trail intersection, the Kruetzer Trail loops around the canyon's south-facing slope. Along this sun-drenched terrain point out examples of plants that have adapted to the climate: evening primrose, yucca, and other cacti. Children enjoy finding other examples. Watch for an aspen tree growing alongside the trail: it may seem out of place here (it is found where the Mount McConnel Trail reconnects), but encourage children to find its source for survival—a spring originating higher in the canyon trickles out at this point on the trail. Stop to enjoy this oasis; within a few feet the trail reenters hot, dry pinyon-juniper country.

Poison ivy and spreading dogbane pepper the trail's final 0.5 mile as it traverses a talus slope. Take time to show children poison ivy's characteristic shiny, deep-green leaves grouped in threes. Children will be interested in learning how dogbane, the compact bush with tiny pink bell-shaped flowers, got its name. It is poisonous if eaten, and its name comes from the Greek words meaning "noxious to dogs."

Just after passing the talus slope, the trail meets the Mountain Park Campground road. Stop here to cool tired feet along the banks of the Poudre River. At the road, turn left and walk 0.2 mile to the trailhead.

Toilet, water, and picnic facilities are available at the adjacent picnic ground.

45. Molly Lake Trail

Location:	Roosevelt National Forest
Type:	Dayhike
Difficulty:	Easy for children
Hikable:	June–October
Distance:	1 mile, one way
Starting elevation:	8600 feet
High point:	8600 feet
Maps:	Roosevelt National Forest, USGS Red Feather Lakes

Driving Directions: From Fort Collins, travel 49 miles northwest on US 287 to Red Feather Lakes. From Red Feather Lakes, turn south on the Manhatten Road and proceed 2.2 miles. The trailhead and parking are on the east side.

The walk to Molly Lake can be experienced as a quiet saunter in the woods or as a lively investigation into the trees that inhabit this diverse forest. The interpreted trail is easy enough for almost anyone and leads to a wet destination kids love—a lake bordered by rocks that the kids will enjoy climbing.

The trail, which starts from the parking lot, follows an old logging road through a soft blend of lodgepole, ponderosa, fir, spruce, and aspen trees. Before leaving the trailhead, pick up the guide sheet available there that contains information corresponding to the numbered posts.

Before leaving, measure a child's hand showing him or her how long 2, 3, 4, and 5 inches are. Then, along the roadway, watch for elk and deer tracks in the mud. Adult deer leave a track 2.5 to 3 inches in length, while an elk's track can reach nearly 5 inches.

Numerous slash piles, the products of forest thinning work, can be seen along the trail. The trees have been cut in an effort to control mountain pine beetle infestation. The flying beetles lay their eggs beneath the bark of the lodgepole and ponderosa pines. The beetle larvae, which feed on a tree's nutrients, carry a fungus that can kill a tree within eighteen months. Woodpeckers, who prefer the beetle for all their meals, usually keep healthy forests safe from beetle infestation.

A core sample has been removed or "bored" from the healthy 240-year-old ponderosa at signpost 2. Kids have fun searching the tree's trunk for the drill hole. Ask them to "measure" the tree's hug circumference, then use that measurement to find a tree half its age, 120 years.

Another method of determining a young tree's age is by 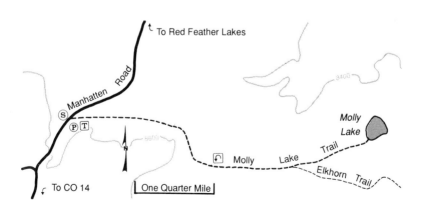 counting the number of branches on one side of the tree. Each

Molly Lake

branch is equivalent to one year. Make up a game in which your companions use this technique to find a tree their own age.

 At signposts 9a and b, children learn how the limber pine got its name. By gently bending the tree's branch, they discover the tree is flexible, another word for limber.

 A halfway mark for little legs is at signpost 14, where views of Lone Pine Valley can be enjoyed while perched on the boulder.

At the trail sign for Elkhorn Creek, veer left for 0.2 mile to Molly Lake. The lake's west side, where boulders are piled among aspens is an ideal picnic spot and rock climbing playground.

Return via the same trail. There are no facilities at the trailhead.

46. Montgomery Pass Trail

Location: Roosevelt National Forest
Type: Dayhike
Difficulty: Moderate for children
Hikable: Mid-June–September
Distance: 1.8 miles, one way
Starting elevation: 10,040 feet
High point: 11,000 feet
Maps: Roosevelt National Forest,
USGS Clark Peak

Driving Directions: From Fort Collins, travel 65 miles west on CO-14. Turn left into the Zimmerman Lake parking lot, located just past the Joe Wright Reservoir.

This is a short, easy walk to a grand expanse of Colorado high country. Like all high-altitude hikes, start this one on a cloudless morn. Doing so gives youngsters ample time to roam this mountaintop landscape, including stops to investigate the intimate views at their feet.

To find the trailhead to Montgomery Pass, from the parking lot, cross the road and follow the edge of timber north for approximately 0.25 mile before entering the forest. Watch for blue plastic

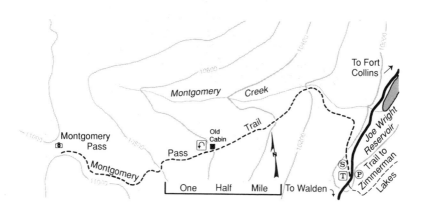

ski trail markers on the trees. Initially, the trail traverses a marshy area and parallels the highway for 0.25 mile before it joins an old logging road. The climb begins as the trail enters a forest of stately spruce trees.

Stop to feel the sharp, pointed needles of spruce trees, which many children say "look just like Christmas trees!" As the trail climbs higher, point out the spruces' cones, dangling from the tree like so many Christmas ornaments. Resident squirrels treat the cones like gift-wrapped presents, tearing them open in search of seeds. The resourceful rodents store their winter cache beneath the shredded cone pile, called a "midden." Find the animals' entry hole into the midden.

At 0.8 mile, watch for the remains of a log cabin on the right. Bear to the right, continuing to a creek crossing. Another 0.5 mile beyond here the tree line gives way to the expanse of alpine tundra. The trail is not easy to discern, but follow in the direction of the pass. Alpine vegetation is extremely slow growing so remind youngsters that all plants and rocks must remain as they are found.

At the top, encourage youngsters to feel the wind's power by standing tall, stretching out their arms. When they inspect the tiny wildflowers, best seen from their hands and knees, they'll understand why these diminutive beauties keep a low profile. If during their exploration, someone smells a skunk, they've discovered sky pilot. This alpine flower cluster with lavender-blue bell-shaped blossoms attracts bees who favor the color. Sedge, a family of grass-like plants, carpets much of the tundra here. Ask children to find sedge by searching for grass that is three-sided and solid. During these close searches, caution children from accidently injuring their eyes on these upright spiky grasses.

Return via the same trail. Toilet and water facilities are available at the trailhead.

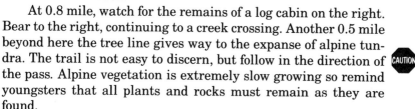

A close encounter with a mushroom

47. Lake Agnes

Location:	Colorado State Forest
Type:	Dayhike or cabin overnight
Difficulty:	Moderate for children
Hikable:	Mid-June–September
Distance:	1 mile, one way
Starting elevation:	10,200 feet
High point:	10,663 feet
Maps:	Colorado State Forest,
	USGS Mount Richtofen,
	USGS Clark Peak

Driving Directions: From Fort Collins, travel west on CO-14 approximately 72 miles to Cameron Pass. Continue 2.6 miles beyond the pass to the gravel road turnoff on the left. A sign for Agnes and American lakes and Crags Campground is posted just before the road. Continue 0.6 mile to the stop sign and booth where State Forest vehicle permits are purchased. Turn right and proceed 1.3 miles up this very steep, two-wheel-drive road. Parking is at the road's end.

The short hike to this clear, forest-fringed jewel in the high country is an alpine odyssey available to most every hiker. Early

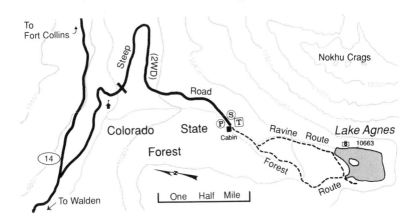

Lake Agnes

in the hike the trail forks, providing a route for both ambitious, rock-scrambling hikers and those drawn to forest serenity. A rustic rental cabin located near the trailhead is a perfect place to overnight in this high-altitude splendor.

From the parking lot, the trail begins behind the cabin on the left side of the creek. Visible from here is the lake's alpine basin rimmed by crags. Point out these rock pinnacle formations, explaining to children that the hike's destination sits below and to the right of them.

Beginning in the spruce forest, the trail crosses a creek before meeting a signpost at 0.3 mile. The trail splits here.

The easier route on the right follows a hushed corridor through towering spruce trees all the way to the lake. The few furred and feathered residents of this high timber area have left their mark. During the walk, encourage youngsters to look and listen for signs of wildlife. Spider webs, woodpecker-dimpled tree trunks, deer scat, and bird calls are among the signs they may find.

Energetic hikers, especially those wearing sturdy hiking shoes, may choose the route on the left, which follows a steep, rocky ravine straight to the lake. The Middle Fork of the Michigan Creek splashes down the ravine's bottom. Look up and to the left where Nokhu Crags pierce the sky like so many stone fingers. Little human hands, however, may prefer to throw snowballs from the snowbanks along the way. Ask children if all the patches of snow will melt away during the summer. Why not? How can the snow here help them find north?

Here and in other high-altitude walks, watch out for pink-tinged "watermelon snow," which if ingested can cause serious digestive upset.

As the trail nears a flattened talus rock area at 0.9 mile, watch for the headgate that steers a portion of the creek into a pipe. This water will eventually flow from water faucets in Fort Collins, nearly 100 miles away.

Both trails meet at the lake where fishing (flies and lures only) or simply rock skipping can be enjoyed.

The recommended return route is via the easier route, the forest trail.

Reservations for renting the rustic cabin, outfitted with beds, table, and a stove for cooking and heating, can be made by calling 1-800-365-2267. Toilet facilities are available behind the cabin. Camping is prohibited at Agnes Lake.

48. Lily Mountain

Location:	Roosevelt National Forest
Type:	Dayhike
Difficulty:	Moderate for children
Hikable:	Mid-April–October
Distance:	3 miles, one way
Starting elevation:	8800 feet
High point:	9786 feet
Maps:	Roosevelt National Forest, USGS Longs Peak

Driving Directions: From Estes Park, go south on CO-7 about 6 miles. Watch for the Mary's Lake Power Plant sign and continue

2.4 miles. A small parking area is available on the shoulder of the road, on the west side where the trail begins.

Lily Mountain is an ideal first ascent for beginning climbers and their parents. This 1000-foot climb requires just enough huffing 'n' puffing followed by a bit of route finding and a short, but fun, rock scramble to the top. As in every good climb, views from the summit are most rewarding. Those who time their walk for the predawn hours may be rewarded with a spectacular sunrise viewed from the summit, plus a cool, solitary hike.

The climb begins directly from the trailhead at the parking area. The first 0.7 mile parallels the highway as it ascends the ridge. Limber pines interspersed with imposing rock groups decorate the slope.

Stop at the pines to let children carefully bend the trees' branches. Explain that limber is another word for flexible. Have them count the number of needles in a bundle. Limber pines are the only Colorado tree bearing five-needle bundles. Further up the trail they will find a similar tree with needles that grow in groups of two—the lodgepole.

The trail continues heading north, passing another trail junction at 1 mile, following a gently rolling grade as it reaches an overlook of the Estes Valley at 1.2 miles. This boulder-shaded spot is an ideal destination for very young mountaineers.

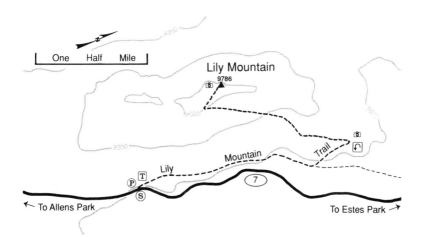

View of Longs Peak from the top of Lily Mountain

From here the trail heads south, climbing steadily through a gallery of lodgepole pines. (Remember to count needles in a bundle.) Note the yellow, flowering, fleshy plants splashing, like drops of sunshine, across an otherwise dry and dull forest. Examine the leaves of this plant, called stonecrop. When a leaf is squeezed, water oozes out—the plant's method of conserving water for life in a very dry home.

The challenge of route finding comes into practice as the trail nears the summit. Look to the right to see Lily Mountain's peak, which consists of a rock pile. Cairns mark the route to the top, which is a fun exercise for most any hiker who comes this far.

The view from the top includes Twin Sisters to the south. Turning to the right you'll see Meadow and St. Vrain Mountains, Longs Peak, and to the northwest, the Mummy Range.

Return via the same route. Bring plenty of water—there are no facilities here.

49. Bear Lake and Glacier Gorge Loops

Location:	Rocky Mountain National Park
Type:	Dayhike
Difficulty:	Easy and moderate, respectively, for children
Hikable:	June–October
Distance:	0.5 mile, loop; or 5.6 miles, loop
Starting elevation:	9475 feet
High point:	10,220 feet
Maps:	Rocky Mountain National Park brochure/map, USGS McHenrys Peak

Wheelchair accessible but assistance may be needed

Driving Directions: From Rocky Mountain National Park's Beaver Meadows entrance station on US 36 near Estes Park, travel 9 miles on the Bear Lake Road to the parking lot for Bear Lake. The trailhead is at the west end of the parking lot. A fee is required to enter the national park and a backcountry use permit is required for all overnight stays.

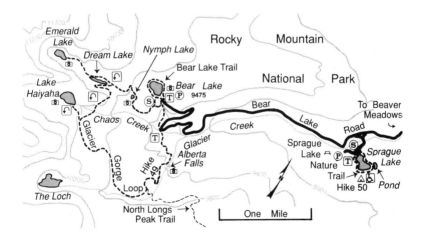

Limber Pine at Dream Lake

You'll enjoy a walk through a collage of nature's best: rainbow-making waterfalls, wildflower-laced streams, cathedral-like forests, and mountain-mirroring lakes. Little wonder the trails near Bear Lake are Rocky Mountain National Park's most popular. A camera is almost essential for this venture.

Crowds can be avoided by starting the hike early in the morning. To lessen the impact of vehicular traffic on this fragile beauty, at the time of this writing a free mass transit system connects Bear Lake with the shuttle parking lot immediately west of the Glacier Basin Campground, 4.8 miles from the start of Bear Lake Road.

For a level, paved introduction, start the hike on the 0.5-mile interpreted loop around Bear Lake. A self-guiding trail booklet detailing the ecology of this typical high-country lake is available at the trailhead. (People in wheelchairs may require assistance on portions of the Bear Lake loop trail.)

Young hikers interested in hiking all or portions of the Glacier Gorge Loop will want to continue on the 0.5-mile paved walkway to Nymph Lake. Along this walk through a lodgepole forest, point out the scarred tree trunks—indicators that a porcupine dined on its bark.

At lily pad–blanketed Nymph Lake, follow the trail around the lake to the viewpoint where Hallet Peak and Flattop Mountain add a grand background to your photographs. Have children examine the wind-sculpted roots of the toppled spruce trees here. Ask "What made the tree fall? Why hasn't the park service removed the tree? How do fallen trees help forest animals?"

Wildflowers and mini-waterfalls edge the 0.5-mile walkway to Dream Lake. On rainy days, of which there are many come midsummer, this mist-shrouded destination reminds me of a Japanese watercolor. Just 0.7 mile beyond here lies Emerald Lake, sparkling and still in its glacial cirque. Rock scramblers of all sizes have fun at this point where the trail ends.

To complete all or portions of the remaining 5-mile Glacier Gorge Loop, head back to Dream Lake where the trail heads south 1.1 miles to Lake Haiyaha. Several switchbacks through dense subalpine fir forest (most years snow covers the path until July) lead to a sun-drenched viewpoint of Nymph and Bear lakes. Longs Peak looms ahead. The trail then follows a relatively level route for 0.25 mile, through limber pines before meeting the short spur to Lake Haiyaha on the right. There's a lonely limber pine here, twisted and gnarled by weather's unyielding forces. A more numerous resident here, Clark's nutcracker, a bold gray bird, will literally grab your children's attention and any food they may be carrying. Remember to honor park regulations by not feeding these "camp robbers."

From the lake, the trail leads 1.2 miles down rocky terrain passing the trail to The Loch on the right. Turn left at the Glacier Gorge Trail signs. On your right, you'll see and hear the roaring, foaming Glacier Creek, which is on display at Alberta Falls, 1.3 miles farther north. Within 0.5 mile, you pass the North Longs Peak Trail, where the absence of trees is obvious, especially on a cloudless summer day. A forest fire in 1900 destroyed the trees, leaving behind dry turf. The cliffs to your left are called Glacier Knobs.

Alberta Falls, a classic aspen-clad watershow, attracts hordes of hikers who have approached it on the 0.6-mile stretch starting at Glacier Gorge Junction. After a photo stop here, continue walking downhill 0.6 mile to the Glacier Gorge trailhead and parking lot. From here take the shuttle bus back to the starting point at Bear Lake, or continue walking another 0.4 mile to the Bear Lake parking lot.

50. Sprague Lake Nature Trail

Location:	Rocky Mountain National Park
Type:	Day hike or overnight camp
Difficulty:	Easy for children
Hikable:	June–October
Distance:	0.5 mile, loop
Starting elevation:	8710 feet
High point:	8710 feet
Map:	Rocky Mountain National Park map/brochure

Wheelchair accessible

Driving Directions: See directions for hike 49, Bear Lake Trail. Parking for Sprague Lake Trail and its picnic area is 0.5 mile south of the Bear Lake Shuttle Bus parking area. A fee is required to enter the national park and a permit is required for use of the wheelchair-accessible campsites.

A hands-on lesson about Rocky Mountain bighorn sheep

This shallow lake is a quiet showpiece of Rocky Mountain National Park's ever-evolving forests and shores. Descriptions of these changes in the trail brochure (available at the trailhead) help parents guide children to certain discoveries along the way. Anglers of all ages appreciate the lake's healthy brook trout population. The first half of the trail is wheelchair accessible and leads to a campsite designed for people in wheelchairs.

For little ones, the lake's first attraction is the resident ducklings paddling around their mothers. Father ducks are the ones with a showy green head atop a white collar. They are commonly seen during the spring nesting season. When the ducks dip their heads into the water, their long, specially adapted tongues are straining food (insects, tiny bits of plants, seeds, fish eggs) from the mud.

As the trail continues edging the lake's north shore, point out in the adjacent forest examples of charred wood—remnants of the fire of 1900, a blaze that nearly destroyed life in the Glacier Creek area. The hearty ponderosa pine trees here survived thanks to their thick bark. Look for knots in the tree to show the bark's thickness. Aspens are newcomers in a forest, the first trees to sprout from their already established roots after a fire has cleared an area.

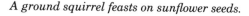

The little brown pond on your left (about 30 yards past the fishing pier) that appears lifeless is actually home for many insects. Its prettiest resident, the brilliant blue-green dragonfly, is a favorite meal of another resident—the frog. Encourage children to watch the dragonfly define its hunting ground, darting after any would-be intruders with the clatter of wings. Kids of all ages are especially fond of dragonflies when they learn this iridescent-colored insect hunts mosquitoes—eating its own weight of them in a half hour! How many mosquitoes could that be?

Before passing by the pond, point out the mosses and grasses taking root around it. Explain that as plants invade this wet area, they deplete the water but build soil as they die and decay over the years. Larger plants eventually take root. When your kids return here with their own children they may find an aspen grove instead of moss!

The entrance to the wheelchair-accessible campsite is just beyond the pond, before the footbridge. On the other side of this creek draining into the lake, take a moment to enjoy great views of the Continental Divide.

As the trail heads back from the footbridge, it winds through

A ground squirrel feasts on sunflower seeds.

a mixed forest. Make a game of identifying each tree by its needles. Lodgepole pine needles come in 1- to 2-inch-long bundles of two and ponderosa pine needles are 3 to 10 inches long in groups of two or three. Engelmann Spruce needles are Stiff and Spiky and subalpine Fir needles are Flat and Flexible.

The trail loops back to its starting point. Wheelchair-accessible toilet and water facilities are available at the Sprague Lake parking lot.

51. Ute Trail Tundra Walk

Location:	Rocky Mountain National Park
Type:	Dayhike
Difficulty:	Moderate for children
Hikable:	Late June–September
Distance:	0.5 mile, one way, to 4 miles, one way
Starting elevation:	11,796 feet
High point:	10,758 feet
Maps:	Rocky Mountain National Park mapbrochure, USGS Fall River Pass

Driving Directions: From the Beaver Meadows entrance station of Rocky Mountain National Park near Estes Park, take Trail Ridge Road for 22 miles to the Alpine Visitor Center. Park at the visitor center. A fee is required to enter the national park.

This hike starts "on top of the world," a vast, alpine parkland speckled with miniature flowers, canopied by a mountain-rimmed skyscape. As the trail descends into the comforting confines of conifer stands, hikers discover dramatic changes in plants and weather. Families with children of mixed ages and abilities can begin their tundra hike together, then, while one adult completes the hike with older kids, the other adult heads back and drives to Milner Pass parking area where the trail ends.

The trail begins in the grassland adjacent to the highway

Checking out alpine flowers above the tree line

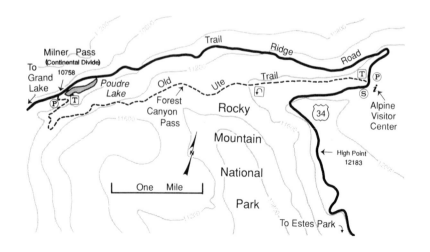

A large bull elk with full rack

crossing. Remember, the tundra ecosystem is extremely delicate; stay on the path at all times. As in all high-altitude hikes, start this one very early to avoid afternoon lightning storms.

Wind makes itself well known as you walk the tundra stretch of the Old Ute Trail, named for the most recent tribe of Indians to use this route to cross the mountains. Alpine flowers and grasses are well adapted to the relentless wind; they remain tiny. Encourage youngsters to experience this adaptation by lying down. Ask if the air feels warmer at this level. Have them measure the tallest flower using their finger as a ruler.

This first 0.5 mile of tundra passes several different ecosystems. Point out small slopes littered with rocks. Explain that these areas, called "fellfields," are really alpine deserts. They receive only 2 to 3 inches of precipitation a year; wind blows them free of snow and rain. Search the rocks for plants surviving these meager conditions. Moss campion, a roundish cushion of tiny leaves, is the plant you're likely to find. Children and adults are awed when they learn it took ten years for this "pioneer" plant to produce its dainty, pink blossoms.

Snowbanks support another community of plants. Have children look for yellow buttercups blooming right through the snow. Nearby might be an alpine marsh. Its wet soil supports willow, a favorite food for browsing elk. Alpine investigators can determine if "wapiti" have frequented the shrub by finding such elk evidence as nibbled leaves and stems, or the animal's dry, brown pellets. Very young hikers may want to turn back after exploring this first 0.5 mile of tundra.

When the road is out of sight, within the first mile, look up and southeast for a great view of Longs Peak, the park's tallest at 14,225 feet. Look west to see the Never Summer Range. These peaks were named by Arapaho Indians and describe the never-melting snowbanks on their eastern slope.

 As the trail continues its descent, stop periodically to measure the increasingly taller grasses and flowers. The dwarfed, wind-sculpted trees near the ponds at 1 mile are a good place to ask "From which direction does the wind blow here?" Size is deceiving at high altitudes; these spruces may well be more than 100 years old.

 At 1.6 miles, in Forest Canyon Pass, bright red Indian paintbrush signals the start of lush wildflower gardens. Watch for lavender flowered "chiming bells" arching 2 feet over the trail. Observant hikers will remember admiring a 3-inch version of it flowering in the tundra portion of their walk.

 The trail winds through a large stand of Christmas tree–sized spruces before making its final 0.5-mile zigzag descent into what is called a "climax forest." Explain that the towering firs and spruces here represent the last stage of plant succession. If a fire were to destroy this forest, grasses, flowers, and aspens would be the first to blanket the slopes. Within 100 years, the "climax trees" would dominate.

At the Milner Pass parking lot, use a highway map to show children they have reached the Continental Divide. Ask "If a drop of rain falling on my left (south) is destined for the Pacific Ocean, where will the rain falling on my right (north) end up?"

52. Deserted Village

Location: Roosevelt National Forest
Type: Dayhike or backpack
Difficulty: Moderate for children
Hikable: June–October
Distance: 3 miles or farther, one way
Starting elevation: 7800 feet
High point: 8200 feet
Maps: Roosevelt National Forest,
USGS Glen Haven

Driving Directions: From Estes Park, drive 6 miles north on the Devils Gulch Road to Glen Haven. Continue 2 miles past the little town to the Dunraven Road, a graveled road on the left. Proceed 2.4 miles to the Forest Service parking lot on the left. The North Fork trailhead begins in the open, grassy slope here. A back-country permit is required for camping within Rocky Mountain National Park boundaries.

Easy access, a scenic trail, excellent fishing, and an historic destination are a few reasons why a hike to the Deserted Village, located just outside of Rocky Mountain National Park, is an ideal

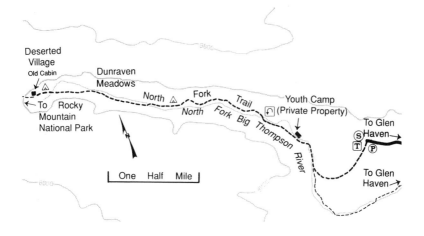

family venture. The trail is part of the North Fork Trail, which leads through beautiful backpacking country along the North Fork of the Big Thompson River.

The trail begins by traversing the hillside before it gently descends through a quietly shaded Douglas-fir and blue spruce forest. The big creek at 0.3 mile is the North Fork of the Big Thompson River. Pass the Glen Haven trailhead on the left, following the Deserted Village trail on the right. As the lush canyon widens, you'll cross the river twice before reaching the private land of a youth camp. The 1-mile trek to the camp can serve as a pleasant destination for tired little legs. Remind hikers to stay on the trail (right of the river) as they pass private property.

Just a few yards beyond the camp, the trail crosses the creek and joins an old four-wheel-drive road briefly. During late July and August, alert young berry pickers to raspberry bushes flourishing on sun-splashed creeksides.

Another food, though certainly less edible-looking, hangs in this forest year-round. Called "black tree lichen," it dangles from spruce limbs in clumps of stringy moss. Children, who are apt to call it "old man's beard" or "witch's hair," are surprised to learn that this lichen was a common food for Indians. They prepared it by soaking it in water then baking it, sometimes with wild onions, in a fire pit. This lichen, which gets its nourishment from particles in the air, doesn't harm the tree.

At 2.5 miles, the trail enters a beautiful, flower-dappled pasture at one time called Dunraven Meadows. The area was named for the earl of Dunraven, an Englishman who more than 100 years ago tried to dishonestly gain title to Estes Park and the Big Thompson River drainage. All that remains of his hunting lodge is the seven-log-tall cabin nestled near the creek in the meadow's west end. Leaving this historic site undisturbed, allow children to examine the structure, looking for modern stabilization techniques.

Backpackers who continue their trek for 1 mile beyond the Deserted Village enter Rocky Mountain National Park where backcountry camping permits are required.

There are no toilet or water facilities at the trailhead.

A young hiker discovers berries on a sunny creekside.

53. Never Summer Ranch

Location: Rocky Mountain National Park

Type: Dayhike

Difficulty: Easy for children

Hikable: Mid-June–October

Distance: 0.5 mile, one way

Starting elevation: 9000 feet

High point: 9020 feet

Maps: Rocky Mountain National Park brochure map

Wheelchair accessible

Driving Directions: From Kawuneeche Visitor Center at the Rocky Mountain National Park's Grand Lake entrance, travel 11.5 miles north on US 34. Turn left on the gravel drive to the parking lot for Never Summer Ranch. A fee is required to enter the national park.

The original homestead and landscape of Never Summer Ranch tell the story of early dude ranching in Colorado. For children, it's the story of a rusted bear trap and a stuffed deer, a hand-operated washing machine, and a foot-pumped sewing machine. It's an encounter with turn-of-the-century ranch life.

The 0.5-mile walk to the cabins and lodge of Never Summer Ranch begins from the parking lot. Visitors arriving at 10:00 A.M.

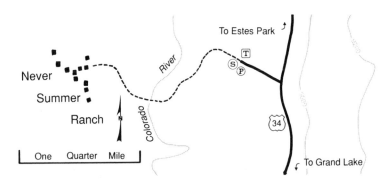

and 2:00 P.M. meet a ranger here for an interpreted tour. The guided walk includes the natural history of Kawuneeche Valley and the story of homesteading this mountain frontier. At the ranch, which consists of the Holzworth family's original cabins, taxidermy shop, ice house, and woodshed, the story is told of a homestead turned dude ranch for tourists.

For those who miss the guided tours, interpreters are on hand from 10:00 A.M. to 4:00 P.M. at the Holzworth grounds answering questions and prompting kids in the homestead experience.

Rusty farm implements grace the grassy meadow surrounding the parking lot. To children, these farm tools are for climbing; to the Holzworths, they were for haying. Horses pulled these rakes to collect and bale the Holzworths' timothy hay, grown here in the Kawuneeche Valley.

The "creek" crossed here is the Colorado River, a babe compared to the raging adult that powers through the Grand Canyon 500 miles south. Johnny Holzworth was one of the first homesteaders to use Colorado River water for irrigation. Children prefer to use this ankle-deep stream for wading.

The short, wide drive leads to the Holzworths' cluster of cabins and outbuildings. A walk through the "Mama" cabin, built in

An old farm implement at Never Summer Ranch

1917, provides a look at how Sophie (Mama) prepared scrumptious meals for her guests using a wood stove and a water pump. Her aprons and bonnets still hang from a kitchen hook.

At the ice house, point out the sod roof. Ask "Why wasn't a wood roof used? Where did the ice come from?" (The Never Summer Range, with its perennial snow patches, was a good source.)

The adjacent taxidermy shop is a popular place to take photographs of children dressed in a buffalo robe and top hat or a lady's bonnet. Trapping apparatus and a stuffed deer are the remnants of Papa's taxidermy trade. Papa used taxidermy to make ends meet after a tractor accident barred him from farm work.

Encourage youngsters to investigate the purpose of the wooden spring box found behind the shop near the creek. The wooden wheelbarrow and wringer washer are among the implements of history children have fun with at Never Summer Ranch.

The cabins are not adapted for wheelchair entry although the driveway around them is level and smooth. Visitors with ambulatory problems who need drive-in access should notify park officials at 303-627-3471 prior to arrival.

54. Adams Falls and East Inlet Trail

Location:	Rocky Mountain National Park
Type:	Day hike or backpack
Difficulty:	Easy to moderate for children
Hikable:	Mid-June–September
Distance:	0.3 mile, one way, to Adams Falls; 5.5 miles, one way, to Lone Pine Lake
Starting elevation:	8400 feet
High point:	9400 feet
Maps:	Rocky Mountain National Park brochure/map, USGS Shadow Mountain

Driving Directions: From US 34 in Grand Lake, turn east on CO-278. At 0.3 mile, the road divides. Take the left fork, which bypasses the town and leads directly to Adams Tunnel. Continue on this paved road 2.1 miles passing the West Portal. Turn left on the graveled road to the trailhead parking lot. A fee is required to enter the national park and a backcountry permit is required for camping.

East Inlet Trail offers a short stroll to Adams Falls or a longer meander through the lush valley spilling into Grand Lake. Beyond the falls, hikers follow a gently rolling grade to a number of worthy destinations: a beaver-worked meadow followed by a number of mountain vistas, a flower-fringed stream, and a lake with an island.

Lodgepole pines and aspens shade the popular 0.3-mile walkway to Adams Falls. Before reaching the falls, hold on to little ones' hands; there are no guardrails here and the surrounding smooth rocks tend to be wet and slippery. On sunny mornings, point out the rainbow arched over the waterfall's spray.

Beyond the falls, the trail follows a level route 0.3 mile through lodgepole pines to a marshy meadow—a favorite home for mosquitoes. Everyone's pace naturally quickens here, and soon the trail enters another stand of lodgepoles before reaching a very large meadow at 0.7 mile. Ask children what animal has changed the land and streamflow. In what ways? What trees probably grew here before the beavers arrived? Does it appear that they still live here? Look for aspen stumps with a chiseled

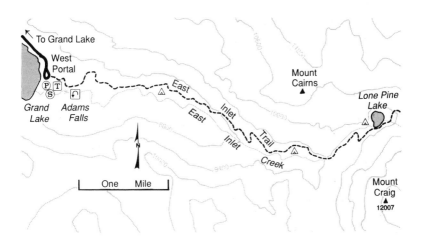

Adams Falls on East Inlet Creek

conical shape. Encourage children to feel the teeth marks made by this timber harvester. The beaver's teeth, unlike our own, continue to grow, and in the process of gathering its food and lodging, the rodent keeps its incisors trim!

From the beaver-designed meadow you have a fine view of Mount Craig, 12,007 feet high. Then, the trail crosses a stream twice and gains altitude slowly as it climbs up and down through more lodgepoles. Within 0.5 mile, it briefly switches back on the slope of Mount Cairns, topping off at a rock shelf where more mountain views can be enjoyed.

The trail continues its rising and falling route, dipping close to flower-laced East Inlet Creek along the last mile to Lone Pine Lake. Hikers intending a lakeside overnight can continue, climbing the switchbacks through thick stands of spruce trees leading to Lone Pine Lake, 5.5 miles from the trailhead. The lake's namesake, a singular lodgepole pine rooted in the rock island, has surrendered to weather's forces. However, it's been replaced by a group of brave young pines and an Engelmann spruce.

Return is via the same trail. Toilet and water facilities are available at the trailhead.

---

55. Blue Lake Trail

Location:	Roosevelt National Forest
Type:	Dayhike
Difficulty:	Easy to moderate for children
Hikable:	Mid-June–September
Distance:	1 mile, one way, to Mitchell Lake; 2.4 miles, one way, to Blue Lake
Starting elevation:	10,470 feet
High point:	10,720 feet at Mitchell Lake; 11,320 feet at Blue Lake
Maps:	Roosevelt National Forest, USGS Ward

Driving Directions: From Boulder, travel 20 miles west on CO-119 to CO-72 near Nederland. Turn right, heading north on CO-72 to Ward. Turn left at the road for Brainard Lake, driving 5.7 miles to the trailhead parking area. Dayhikers leave their cars here. Backpackers have a designated parking area close to Brainard Lake. The trailhead for Blue Lake Trail is on the southwest (left) side of the parking lot.

The walk to Mitchell Lake is a tranquil meander through a stately subalpine forest. Children find it fairy-tale charming as

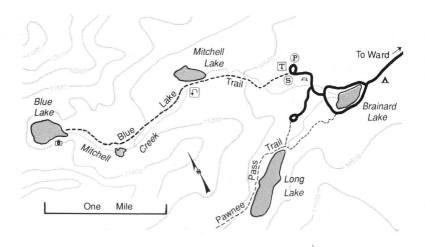

they discover rock gnomes and flower angels along the way. The brisk trek to Blue Lake edges a year-round snowbank before reaching the waterfall-fed lake, which remains frozen until mid-summer.

The wide path leaves the parking lot, entering a cathedral-quiet stand of senior subalpine *F*irs. Have children feel the *F*lat, *F*lexible fingers (needles) of this grandfather tree. Compare them to the firs' frequent companion, the Engelmann *S*pruce, which bears *S*quare and *S*piky needles.

At 0.4 mile, a footbridge spans the raging Mitchell Creek, then enters the Indian Peaks Wilderness. Roots and rocks, which make for good gnome-hunting territory, rubble the trail, requiring careful footing. Point out how the silent forest inhabitants have painted their rock homes with lichen. Encourage youngsters to find different colors and textures of lichen. Kids of all ages remember how this half-algae, half-fungus plant is formed when the following story is told: When Alice Algae met Freddy Fungus they decided they had a lichen for each other. The two married, but now their relationship is on the rocks! The *real* story—that the algae portion of lichen produces food for the plant, while the fungus part serves as a rock-attaching, water-holding structure—appeals to hikers, not gnome hunters.

Flower fairies abound where the trail reaches the creek draining into Mitchell Lake at 1 mile. Take time to introduce

Spruce have square and spiky needles.

children to some of the subalpine forest's prettiest flower maid-
ens. Tall (12 to 18 inches) and slender, Parry's primrose wears a
cluster of pink-red blossoms atop its lean stem. Another one in
pink is rose crown with rows of fleshy leaves. Little red elephant
wears a chorus line of elephants' heads, each one saying hello
with its trunk raised high. White marsh marigold is a wall
flower, blooming close to banks of snow.

Hikers continuing to Blue Lake climb the Mitchell Creek
drainage for 1 mile before reaching a snowbank at tree line. In
early summer, the trail hides under winter's blanket; by mid-July
it skirts to the right of the snow.

Blue Lake also wears a winter coat through most of the summer. However, it is a worthy summer destination to see the lake's
waterfall cascading 500 feet into the northwest shore and Mount
Toll soaring 1600 feet above the water.

Return via the same trail. Toilet, water, and picnic facilities
are available at the day-use parking lot.

56. Fish Creek Falls

Location: Routt National Forest
Type: Dayhike
Difficulty: Easy for children
Hikable: May–October
Distance: 0.3 mile, one way
Starting elevation: 7440 feet
High point: 7340 feet
Maps: Routt National Forest,
USGS Steamboat Springs
Wheelchair accessible

Driving Directions: From Steamboat Springs, travel 4.1 miles east on Fish Creek Road, located at the south end of town on US 40.

Waterfalls such as Fish Creek Falls are irresistible. Two trails lead to this spectacular water cascade. One takes a down-

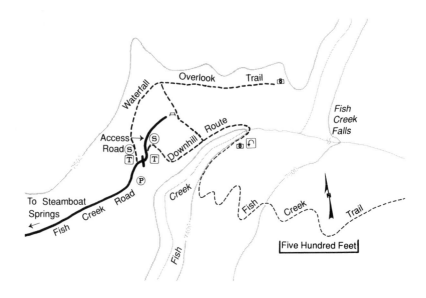

Stream play at Fish Creek Falls

hill route to the rock-strewn creek below the falls where children climb and explore for hours. The other, a paved, wheelchair-accessible trail, weaves through some of nature's finest forest varieties, ending at the waterfall overlook.

The downhill route to the falls begins at the parking lot's east end, to the right of the access road. After a brief, steep descent, a spur trail on the left leads to the restroom and picnic area. The trail levels off just beyond here, edging Fish Creek.

The roar of water thundering 283 feet down a rock-choked cliff 0.1 mile off spurs youngsters to run ahead. Keep an eye on them; the large bridge spanning Fish Creek looks like a jungle gym to little climbers. Photographs taken here of kids and the waterfall may need to wait until after young explorers have scouted the site. This is a destination children resist leaving.

The falls, your explorers may want to know, spill over what is called a hanging valley. During the Ice Age, more than a million years ago, a small glacier and a huge glacier joined here. Over thousands of years the glaciers melted. In doing so, the large one eroded great amounts of rock material under it. The little glacier scoured out only a shallow valley high above the larger one. The cliff under the waterfall marks the place where the glaciers met.

From the bridge, the Fish Creek Trail continues heading east to a number of lake destinations. Fewer people are encountered along this trail the farther it is hiked.

The paved path to the waterfall overlook starts at the parking lot's north side. Interpretive brochures are available (donation requested) at the trailhead.

 The variety of trees and shrubs growing along this 1500-foot path reminds me of a forest dweller's deli. Encourage children to watch for the different foods animals may eat. Some of their finds may include acorns of the scrub oak, a wild rose's flower and fruit, thimbleberry (similar to raspberry), service berry (the fruit of a tree with round, serrated leaves), the winged seeds of the Rocky Mountain maple, the blue berry of a juniper tree, or even a dandelion. What food is most plentiful? What animal eats it? When do the animals come to eat here?

 At the approach to the overlook hold on to little ones' hands. Return via the same trail.

57. Mad Creek Trail

Location:	Routt National Forest
Type:	Dayhike or backpack
Difficulty:	Moderate for children
Hikable:	Mid-May–October
Distance:	1.7 miles, one way
Starting elevation:	6763 feet
High point:	7140 feet
Maps:	Routt National Forest, USGS Mad Creek, USGS Rocky Peak

Driving Directions: From Steamboat Springs, turn north on the Elk River Road and drive 5.7 miles, just past the village of Mad Creek. A buck-and-pole fence borders the parking lot on the right.

This diversely forested trail gently climbs above Mad Creek's fuming torrent until it meets the stream in a calm meadow. Here, children delight in boulder hopping across the creek or teasing its waters with a fishing pole. Mad Creek Trail is one of the area's first hikes to enjoy in spring.

The trailhead is on the parking lot's north side, just across from the private drive. Rumbling in the darkly vegetated crevice to the right is Mad Creek.

As the trail edges along the south-facing slope and rises above private property, point out the plants of this dry, gravelly terrain: yucca, oak, sage, juniper, and pinyon. Evening primrose, a lovely, white-petaled, ground-hugging flower, is among the prettiest of dry land flora to be found here. Watch for a primrose in its closed bud stage. When one is found, let a child feel the plant respond to his or her hands held carefully cupped around the unopened flower. Under the best of conditions (warm hands held for at least five minutes), the flower petals open. This sensation makes the hike unforgettable.

Within 0.5 mile, the trail veers north topping a steep canyon of spruce and fir trees. Along the left side point out the exposed roots of mighty conifers towering overhead. Ask children why the trees are tipped sideways. Why is the soil gone from around the roots? What can be done to prevent more soil erosion? To the right are numerous spots to peek out over the canyon to see Mad Creek's waterfalls spilling a white, lacy ribbon, 200 feet below. However, use caution in selecting these viewpoints; there are sev- eral sheer dropoffs along the way.

At 1.2 miles, the trail enters another oak and sage area then descends gradually into a lovely aspen-fringed meadow. Pass

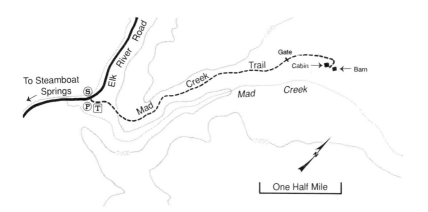

A hiking family planning an extended trip

through the Forest Service gate, staying to the left of the buck-and-pole fence (constructed to protect the stream bank vegetation from grazing animals). Follow the trail through a grassy meadow with a cabin and an old barn in the background. At 1.5 miles, turn right at the sign for the Mad Creek guard station and follow the wide path through the meadow before it meets an old road leading to the creek.

A picnic lunch at the mellow grassland surrounding the creek is a pleasant topping to this hike. Fishing is reportedly good at Mad Creek. The nearby barn, home to rodents and hay bits, was built in 1908 and is not designed for eager young explorers. The cabin presently serves as Forest Service employee housing, please respect their privacy.

Dayhikers may want to wander this valley area before returning on the same trail to the trailhead.

A vault toilet is available at the trailhead.

58. Rabbit Ears Peak

Location:	Routt National Forest
Type:	Dayhike
Difficulty:	Moderate to challenging (at ascent) for children
Hikable:	Mid-June–September
Distance:	2.5 miles, one way
Starting elevation:	9590 feet
High point:	10,654 feet
Maps:	Routt National Forest, USGS Rabbit Ears

Driving Directions: From Steamboat Springs, drive 21 miles south and east on US 40 to the turnoff for Dumont Lake Campground, Forest Service road No. 315 (1 mile west of Rabbit Ears Pass). Proceed 1.6 miles, passing the campground, to a large boulder on the left. Turn left on road No. 311 and travel 0.3 mile to four-wheel-drive road No. 291. Park in the clearing alongside the road.

The hike to Rabbit Ears Peak, named for its twin rock pillars visible from the highway, begins as a casual walk through a spec-

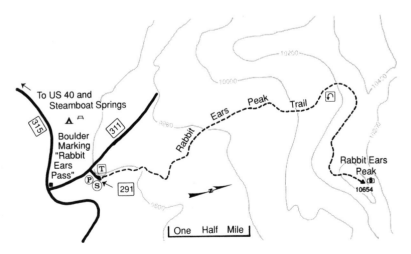

Rabbit Ears Peak Trail is prime columbine country.

tacular flowerland. For some hikers, the last 0.25 mile to the "ears" poses a challenge; to others, it's a fun rock scramble. Either way, the views near the summit are grand.

The trail begins on an old jeep road (motorized vehicles are now prohibited) following an easy grade through what appears to be a carefully orchestrated explosion of colors. Wildflowers of scarlet, pink, yellow, and lavender brighten the field throughout the summer. Locals say they peak in mid-July. However, the flower show during my early August trek to Rabbit Ears is remembered as the summer's best.

A flower guide is useful for such walks, but flower games can be more fun. Encourage children to find their favorite colored flower. Give it a special name. Look for the oddest shaped flower. (Purple monkshood and larkspur are likely candidates.) The prettiest smelling. (Columbine's scent suggests honeysuckle.) The one bees like the best. (Because blue is the favored color of bees, the tall flowering purple-blue penstemon is often the winner.) The tiniest, the biggest, and so on. Remind children to leave the flowers for others (hikers and bees!) to enjoy.

For 1.5 miles, a steady sprinkling of lodgepole pines, spruce, and aspen dots the meadow as the trail makes a wide arc to the left of Rabbit Ears. From this angle, the rock pair no longer looks like a rabbit's ears. The trail then enters a spruce forest before reaching the steep, rocky climb to the peaks. This may be a delightful destination for little ones.

The road ends at the base of Rabbit Ears. Scramble straight up and over the rocks for about 30 feet. Check each handhold; the rocks are not secure. A faint trail on the right loops around a large block of rock (not an "ear"). A causeway between the block and two ears can be walked. The views from this point on the Continental Divide include Walton Peak in the southwest, Indian Pass to the southeast, followed by Carter Mountain and Granny's Nipple. To the north is Round Mountain and the ripple of peaks in the Continental Divide range.

To some, the mounds of lava rock at their feet are more fascinating than the views. Explain that long ago lava erupted from deep within the earth as a hot, liquid rock. Allow children to hold the rock and decide if it feels lighter than most rocks its size. Ask them what caused it to look like a black sponge.

The return route is via the same trail. The adjacent campground facilities include water, toilet, and picnic grounds.

WEST/SOUTHWEST

(Grand Junction, Durango, Mesa Verde)

59. Trail Through Time

Location: Rabbit Valley
Type: Dayhike
Difficulty: Easy for children
Hikable: March–November
Distance: 1.2 miles, loop
Starting elevation: 4700 feet
High point: 4820 feet
Maps: Colorado State Highway map,
Trail Through Time brochure

Driving Directions: From Grand Junction, take I-70 west 30 miles to the Rabbit Valley exit, Exit 2. Turn right and park near the gate. The trail begins 250 feet north from here.

Imagine walking across a dry, windswept, rocky mesa, the drone of an interstate just out of earshot, and discovering dinosaur bones! Located only 30 miles west of Grand Junction in Rab-

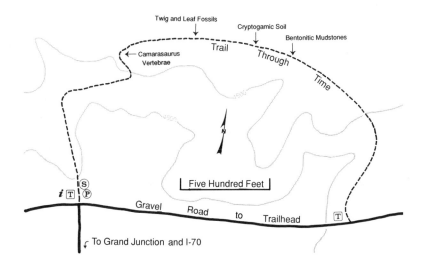

Camarasaurus vertebrae at Trail Through Time

bit Valley, this interpreted stroll through a dinosaur quarry is a rewarding diversion for both dinosaur fans and rock hounds. Considered the southern tip of the Dinosaur Triangle, which extends north to Vernal, Utah, and west to Price, Utah, the Trail Through Time is riddled with fossilized dinosaur bones and plant material.

Before beginning the walk, describe to children that 140 million years ago this high desert was a lush floodplain—a swampy place where dinosaurs roamed and flying reptiles soared. Amidst giant ferns and heavy clouds all that could be heard was the rumble of thunder, the buzz of insects, and the sudden roars of prehistoric creatures. Perhaps the dinosaur devotee of your group can add to the picture.

At the trailhead, an informative sign highlights the geologic history of the Rabbit Valley region. The trail brochure, available in a stand behind here, points out the geological and paleontological sites that might otherwise be overlooked. However, after seeing the 3-foot stretch of Camarasaurus vertebrae imbedded in rock at site 2, most hikers stay tuned for more signs of ancient remnants. Encourage youngsters to examine rocks along the trail, many of which are imprinted with plant fossils, the remnants of a dinosaur's diet. Near signpost 4 are several impressions of twigs and leaves deposited 135 million years ago. Fossils were formed long, long ago when plants or animals were trapped, then buried under layers of dirt and sand (sediment). Over time, the layers turned to rock and the impression made by the plant or animal remained. Are fossils being made now?

 Near signpost 6 take time to examine the dry, sandy soil—it's alive! The black, crusty stuff covering much of the untrampled terrain here is called "cryptogamic soil." It is like a plant, composed of lichen, fungi, mosses, and algae that combine to bind and anchor the loose grains of sand. The spongy crust holds moisture, prevents erosion, and sometimes traps seeds. Plant communities develop from cryptogamic soil. Advise children not to tread on it— this very valuable plant takes years to restore.

On rainy days use caution near signpost 8. Bentonitic mudstone, a decomposed volcanic ash deposited millions of years ago, gets very slippery when wet. Allow children to examine this fine-textured deposit.

At the trail's end, leave the brochure at the stand. From here follow the gravel road 0.2 mile back to the car looking skyward for eagles, hawks, and ravens soaring much higher than flying reptiles once did.

Toilet facilities are available near the trailhead. For more information call 303-243-DINO.

60. Alcove Nature Trail

Location: Colorado National Monument
Type: Dayhike
Difficulty: Easy for children
Hikable: Year-round
Distance: 0.5 mile, one way
Starting elevation: 5787 feet
High point: 5787 feet
Maps: Colorado National Monument brochure

Driving Directions: From Grand Junction, drive 12 miles west on I-70. Take Exit 19 to Fruita, continuing 2 miles on CO-340 to Colorado National Monument's west entrance and pay park entrance fee. Proceed 9 very winding miles to the visitor center parking lot and park headquarters. The Alcove Nature Trail begins just across from the entrance to the visitor center.

As one of the few trails in Colorado National Monument far from a precipitous canyon rim, the Alcove Nature Trail serves as a delightful introduction to desert wildlife and geology. Lizards darting straight up a cliff or a series of "caves" carved into a sandstone wall are among the attractions children like best.

The brochure that accompanies this 31-site interpreted trail has a wealth of interesting information about plant and animal adaptations in this dry environment. Use these facts to direct children's discoveries. For example, try squeezing the sagebrush leaves to discover the desert's fragrance.

Along the way, watch for skunkbrush, with its miniature oak-shaped leaves. It is named for the peculiar odor its foliage gives off when bruised. By mid-June it produces red berries that make mouths pucker like no lemon ever has. The fruit of the skunkbrush is a favorite food for birds and small animals.

At signposts 7 and 8, have kids run their hands across a sandstone outcrop. The granules of sand that remain on their palms came from an ancient coastline that existed near here long, long ago. Encourage them to imagine this dry landscape as it once was, covered with lakes and marshes.

Near the trail's end, at the base of the sandstone wall on the left, wind and water erosion has sculpted miniature caves. Look

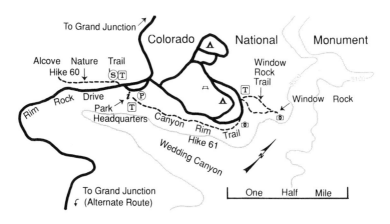

Old juniper at Alcove Nature Trail

 for dimples in the sand here just below the rock overhangs. At the base of these tiny depressions sits a hungry ant lion awaiting an unlucky insect.

 During the summer months another insect predator, the sagebrush lizard, is likely to be seen scampering through the sand near here. Your children can "feel" where this animal prefers to live by placing their hands on sand exposed to direct sunlight and in the shade of a tree.

 During the return hike, ask your children which are more prevalent: trees with leaves or trees with needles. Leaves allow moisture to evaporate, whereas the needles of coniferous trees have a waxy coating that prevents moisture loss—a necessary adaptation for this dry climate.

Leave the trail brochure at the trailhead stand. Water and toilet facilities are available at the visitor center.

61. Canyon Rim and Window Rock Trails

Location: Colorado National Monument
Type: Dayhike
Difficulty: Easy for children
Hikable: Year-round
Distance: 0.7 mile, one way
Starting elevation: 5787 feet
High point: 5787 feet
Maps: Colorado National Monument brochure, USGS Colorado National Monument

Driving Directions: See the directions for hike 60, Alcove Nature Trail.

This ramble through a pinyon-juniper woodland alongside a canyon rim leads to overlook points that most kids say are "really cool."

The Canyon Rim Trail of Colorado National Monument begins at the bottom of the stairs behind the visitor center. From a safe distance the trail parallels Wedding Canyon with a view of Independence Monument, once part of the massive rock wall between Wedding and Independence canyons. Weathering forces eroded most of the wall, leaving behind the remaining freestanding monolith.

Utah juniper, the most common tree here, is best known by man and animals for its frosty blue berries. Explain to children that Indians ground the seeds of the fruit into a flour. Ask a young hiker to crush one of the berries between his or her fingers and discover its distinctive odor. Point out the tree's fibrous bark. Imagine pounding it, as the Ute Indians did, into a soft diaper for babies!

Within 0.5 mile, the trail heads northwest to a car-accessible overlook where panoramic views of the Book Cliffs line the horizon. Why do you think this towering palisade that extends into Utah was named so? From here the sandstone artistry of spires

Odd rock formations as seen from the Canyon Rim Trail

within Colorado National Monument can be viewed. Shaped by wind, water, ice, and heat, only stone fingers remain where a plateau of less weather-resistant rock once stood. Look for the slender monoliths named Kissing Couple, Praying Hands, Pipe Organ. Kids may have different names for the images they see in the formations.

Continue on the brief paved portion of the trail, which overlooks the Book Cliffs. At the base of this formation, the rich farmland called the Grand Valley is serpentined by the Colorado River.

After leaving the Book Cliffs viewpoint, the short route to Window Rock becomes a dirt pathway, not well defined but usually marked by footprints. However, do stay on the trail. Cryptogram, the dark, lumpy crust that anchors this loose soil takes years to reestablish itself after it's been damaged. Allow children a hands-and-knees investigation of this plant community composed of fungi, moss, algae, and lichen.

At 0.7 mile, the "window" of Window Rock appears in the

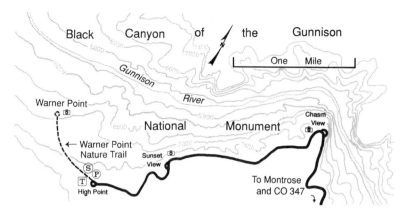

stone wall, seen from behind a fenced point at the trail's end. The window began as a crack and has been carved out over thousands of years by the relentless forces of wind and water erosion.

To return, follow the trail back to the sheltered Book Cliff overlook and continue walking west on the roadside to the parking lot.

62. Warner Point Nature Trail

Location:	Black Canyon of the Gunnison National Monument
Type:	Dayhike
Difficulty:	Easy to moderate for children
Hikable:	May–October
Distance:	0.7 mile, one way
Starting elevation:	8289 feet
High point:	8302 feet
Map:	Black Canyon brochure

Driving Directions: From Montrose, drive 7 miles east on US 50 to the entrance to Black Canyon of the Gunnison National Monument, CO-347, and pay park entrance fee. Turn left, continue 7.3 miles to the visitor center, then proceed another 6.2 miles to the trailhead parking area.

The walk to Warner Point follows a roller-coaster path along a ridge offering awesome views of the Black Canyon. Children love exploring the varied terrain, scrambling up and down each little summit on the trail. Benches along the way serve as destinations for little hikers or as delightful spots from which to enjoy this high desert garden.

The Warner Point Nature Trail guidebook is available at the trailhead. Before going any farther, have children experience the spicy fragrance of sagebrush by rubbing a few of its gray-green leaves between their fingers. From here, the trail begins in a pinyon-juniper stand, many of which are gnarled and twisted by the area's weather extremes. Size can be deceiving under such

The Gunnison River snakes through Black Canyon.

conditions. These trees, though short in stature, are hundreds of years old. What makes them look so old?

Pinyons along the trail bear scars made by porcupines dining on their bark. Watch for trees that are girdled by porcupine gnawings. In such cases, the tree's water and nutrient system has been cut off and the ancient tree will die. Also, because decaying trees are host to a number of insects and animals, the tree will not be removed by park officials.

Another common inhabitant here is the mountain mahogany bush. During summer months, the bush's long, feathery seed tails coil and straighten in response to changes in moisture. Have kids look for seed plumes that have started working their way into the ground.

As you look skyward at signpost 3, the San Juan Mountains etch the horizon. Below them are green, irrigated meadows that contrast with the surrounding dry land.

Near signpost 4, the trail follows a narrow hogback with dizzying views into Black Canyon. (Cliffs and overlooks such as this are not protected by guardrails, so keep an eye on little ones.) From this perspective, children can see why the canyon was named "black." In 1881 the railroad construction crew laying rails for the "Scenic Line" called their workplace the Black Canyon because, they complained, they never saw the sun during their winter's work. The mountain range in the distance is called the West Elks.

While walking toward signpost 6, look to the right for views of the Gunnison River. It took two million years for the river to carve this gorge called Black Canyon.

Just beyond the rest bench at signpost 9, the trail becomes flat as it approaches Warner Point. This wide, open vista allows an unparalleled look at the Gunnison River and the varying rock layers forming this canyon. Be extra watchful here of those who tend to roam.

Return via the same trail, leaving the trail brochure in the box near the trailhead. Toilet facilities are available here.

63. Mesa Lake Shore Trail

Location: Grand Mesa National Forest
Type: Dayhike
Difficulty: Easy for children
Hikable: June–September
Distance: 1 mile, loop
Starting elevation: 9900 feet
High point: 9900 feet
Map: Grand Mesa National Forest

Driving Directions: From Grand Junction, take I-70 for 48 miles east to CO-65 to Mesa. Continue driving 14 miles south of Mesa. Turn west at the Forest Service sign for Mesa Lakes, passing a cabin/resort area and turning left at the bottom of the hill. In 0.5 mile, you will arrive at Glacier Springs Picnic Grounds. The trailhead is at the far end of the parking lot. This trail can also be accessed from the south via Delta and Cedaridge.

The variety of terrains and signs of wildlife surrounding this lake intrigues youngsters of all ages, including their grandpar-

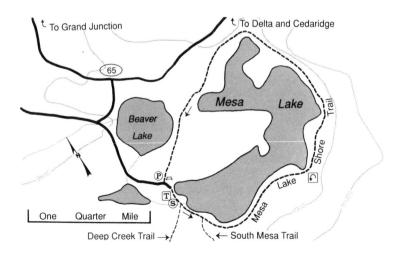

The fishing is great at Mesa Lake.

ents. During my visit to Mesa Lake, I watched several young anglers proudly walk the trail carrying stringers loaded with trout.

From the parking lot, the trail starts at the lake's west shore, which is bordered by a stand of very old and large (some two hugs wide!) spruce and aspen trees. Head to the right, passing within a few yards the sign for Deep Creek Trail, a 1-mile forest trek to a magnificent view on top of Grand Mesa.

In 0.2 mile, after passing a collection of lake-side boulders seemingly placed as fishing chairs, the South Mesa Trail meets

Young rock skippers

the Mesa Lake Shore Trail. Continue to the left. The lake's main water source, Glacier Springs, is on the right. This small pool spills nearly 200 gallons a minute into Mesa Lake. Where does Glacier Springs get its water? When children see that no streams feed into it, explain that a spring results from an underground flow of water.

As the trail edges the lake's southern shore, at 0.4 mile tell children beaver have lived here. Have them look to the right of the trail for beaver signs: a pool of water stilled behind a twig-and-mud dam, aspen stumps with a chiseled conical shape, or perhaps the animal's webbed footprint in the mud.

Along the muddy shores they may discover another water dweller's insignia: a muskrat's set of footprints bisected by a line made as the animal dragged its tail. It is unlikely that the muskrat will make a daytime appearance because it is most active during the evening hours. However, encourage children to find remnants of the muskrat's diet, fragments of grasses and stems floating in shallow water or along the lake edge.

Circling the lake's eastern edge at 0.6 mile, the trail enters the base of a steep slope smothered in boulders. Listen for another animal sign: the high-pitched whistle of a pika or rock rabbit. In late summer, this "haymaker's" winter food, collected in miniature haystacks, may be drying on a rock.

Just beyond the boulder slope, note the young spruce trees growing in the mature aspen stand. The spruce will soon crowd out the aspens. In this way, forests are continually forming.

For the final 0.2 mile, the trail follows a ridge above Beaver Lake and reconnects at the parking lot for Glacier Springs Picnic Grounds. Toilet and water facilities are available here.

---

64. Crag Crest National Recreation Trail

Location:	Grand Mesa National Forest
Type:	Dayhike or backpack
Difficulty:	Moderate to challenging for children
Hikable:	Late June–mid-September
Distance:	1.2 miles, one way, to Forrest Lake; 2 miles, one way, to Crag Crest; or 10 miles, loop
Starting elevation:	10,150 feet
High point:	11,189 feet
Maps:	Grand Mesa National Forest, USGS Grand Mesa

Driving Directions: From Grand Junction or Delta, take CO-65 to Ward Lake Recreation Area in Grand Mesa. Turn east on Forest Road 121, traveling 2.4 miles to the junction of Old Highway 65 (Forest Road 123) and CO-65. Turn north (left) and drive 1.8 miles, passing the Eggleston Lake Campground to the Crag Crest Campground. Parking for hikers is in the lot opposite the campground.

Whether hiked as a gentle walk to a secluded lake or a vigorous climb to a crest on the world's largest flattop mountain, the Crag Crest Trail enables hikers of all abilities to enjoy Grand Mesa, Colorado's evergreen island in the sky.

Starting this trail from the trailhead adjacent to Crag Crest Campground, hikers can take the 2-mile route rising 1000 feet to Crag Crest, a rocky pinnacle surrounded by outstanding mountain vistas. From this viewpoint, the trail follows the ridge line 3.0 miles before it loops back to the trailhead.

Those with shorter legs and less endurance can start their hike with the 10-mile-loop crest climbers and then leave them within 0.1 mile to head west on the mellow 1.2-mile trail to Forrest Lake. (On some USGS maps, this lake is called "Upper Hotel Lake.") The first 0.3 mile of the Forrest Lake trail requires just a bit of exertion before it levels off in an old-growth spruce forest. Clumps of stringy moss hanging from these trees intrigue most hikers. This growth, which some call "old man's beard," is actually named black lichen, at one time an important food for Indians. Try inspiring children to take some lichen home to prepare it the traditional way by stewing it with onions over low heat.

 Time spent splashing in the creek that drains from this forest-fringed lake, followed by a picnic lunch on its shore, is a delightful way to enjoy this destination.

Those hiking to Crag Crest or the entire loop first meet Upper Eggleston Lake, its still waters rippled by jumping trout, followed by Bullfinch Reservoir 0.5 mile farther. Dogtooth violets (or glacier lily), yellow lilies with two long shiny leaves, flower as the snow melts in the forest undergrowth here. This edible plant has a potato-like bulb and a seed pod that when cooked tastes similar to green beans.

After passing the sign for Butts Lake at 1.2 miles, the trail continues heading north, zigzagging a path to the crest. Soon the aspen-fir forest gives way to open, treeless vistas. Stay tuned to the trail here and watch for steep dropoffs on both sides. As the

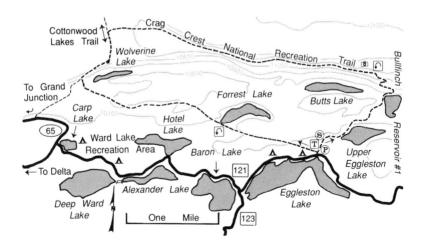

Little red elephants in bloom

trail passes the area covered with lava rock, tell children that the rocks are indicators of the 400-foot-thick lava layer that blanketed this mountain 10 million years ago. Children should test the weight of the porous red-black lava.

The 360-degree view from Crag Crest includes the Book and Roan cliffs to the northwest. The rugged, lava-topped mountain directly north is Battlement Mesa. The highest point to the east is 11,234-foot Leon Peak. Also in this direction are the Elk Mountains and the Anthracite Range. To the south are Gunnison Peak, Uncompahgre Peak, the San Juan Mountains, and Lone Cone. Far to the west are the Uncompahgre Plateau and the LaSal Mountains of Eastern Utah. Some hikers may want to see more of these spectacular views along the ridge west of the crest before heading back on the same trail.

To complete the loop, head west 3 miles on the crest portion of the trail. Turn south onto the Cottonwood Lakes Trail, walking 1.5 miles to the lower 3.5-mile section, which passes Forrest Lake on its return to the trailhead at Crag Crest Campground.

Toilet and water facilities are available at the campground. Mosquito repellent is advised for most hikes on the Grand Mesa.

65. Animas Overlook Trail

Location:	San Juan National Forest
Type:	Dayhike
Difficulty:	Easy for children
Hikable:	May–October
Distance:	0.6 mile, loop
Starting elevation:	8000 feet
High point:	8,080 feet
Map:	San Juan National Forest

Wheelchair accessible

Driving Directions: From the Durango town center, head north on Main Street to 25th Street; turn left (west). Follow this street,

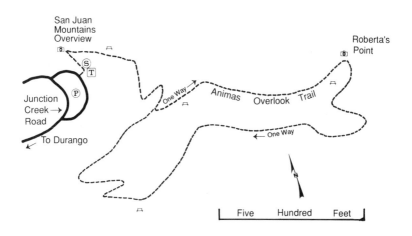

The trailhead at Animas Overlook

also called Junction Creek Road, for 5 miles, where it enters the San Juan National Forest. Continue on this gravel road, called Forest Road 543, to milepost 8 where parking for the Animas Overlook Trail is on the right.

The Animas Overlook Trail is a short, very pleasurable trail that tells of the diverse forces that shaped this corner of the state. Nine interpretive signposts along this wheelchair-accessible path provide the kind of geological, ecological, and historical information that normally requires paging through several guidebooks. This forest trail is rich with signs of wildlife.

From the trailhead, the trail veers left a few yards to the San Juan Mountain Overlook, providing views of the Animas Valley, crowned by the San Juan Mountains to the north, with the Animas River flashing like a huge silver snake through its middle. Point out the river's lazy, winding path through the flat valley below. Ask "Why doesn't the river follow a straight line?"

e Mullein, the tall, woolly "weed" growing beside the trailhead post, is best appreciated by children when they touch its soft leaves against their cheeks. After experiencing the plant in this way, they will understand why the plant is collected for use in making skin-softening lotions.

e As the trail winds through the ponderosa forest, look for charred bark on tree trunks—evidence of the controlled burn here in 1977. You may find conspicuous little piles of de-scaled pinecones set on a tree stump. They are remnants of the chickaree squirrel feeding on the cones' seeds. More often heard than seen, this common reddish-brown squirrel frequently calls from a tree in scolding tsk, tsk, chrrrr notes.

e Another sound heard in this forest is the rat-a-tat drills of a downy woodpecker in search of an insect meal or declaring its property. A woodpecker can beat its head against wood 20 times a second, in uninterrupted bursts for almost an hour! Woodpeckers have special feet to give them a good grip on the tree, and their long, stiff tails help hold them in place.

Other animal signs to look for are the dry pellets of the mule deer left near oak brush. Examine the leaves of this deer forage to see if it has been nibbled on recently. Look skyward where a large black bird might be soaring overhead; it may be a turkey vulture riding a thermal. At dusk, quiet hikers often hear the resonant hoo hoo-oo of a great horned owl.

This recently completed trail is a cooperative project initiated by the area's Business and Professional Women. It was designed and developed by members of the San Juan Forest Service and completed by a crew of developmentally disabled adults from Durango. Ultimately, braille guides will be available for the trail. Wheelchair-accessible parking and toilet facilities are available at the trailhead.

66. Red Creek Trail

Location:	San Juan National Forest
Type:	Dayhike or backpack
Difficulty:	Moderate for children
Hikable:	May–October
Distance:	Up to 3 miles, one way
Starting elevation:	8080 feet
High point:	9856 feet
Maps:	San Juan National Forest, USGS Rules Hill, USGS Durango East, USGS Hermosa

Driving Directions: From Durango, take E. Third Avenue north to its end, bearing right (northeast) on Florida Road. Follow this road 9.6 miles, just past a steep uphill curve where a sign on the left reads "Colvig Silver Camps." Turn left on this wide gravel road and travel almost 2 miles. The road appears to end at the camp's barn building, but continue almost 1 mile farther on this narrow road suitable for two-wheel-drive vehicles in dry weather. Park in the clearing on the right side of the road. The trailhead is behind the cattle fence on the opposite side of Red Creek marked

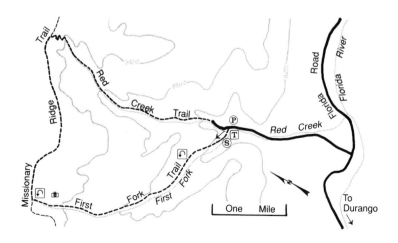

by a small wooden sign for "First Fork." Please remember to close all gates.

The splashing, gurgling sounds of First Fork, the stream that joins Red Creek at the trail's beginning, accompany hikers most of the way to Missionary Ridge. The first 2.5 miles climb gradually, with numerous creek-side destinations along the way. At the top, the trail along Missionary Ridge offers views of the Animas River valley to the northwest, and the Florida River valley to the southwest.

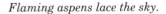 The easy-to-follow trail winds through a narrow, red-walled canyon shaded by towering aspen and spruce. There are numerous environmental investigation opportunities beside the trail that can also serve as turnaround points.

After climbing several short hills, at 0.7 mile, the trail wanders through one of the loveliest aspen stands I've encountered.

Flaming aspens lace the sky.

For a fun perspective on this forest, ask the members of your group to gather around one aspen tree and lie on their backs with their heads touching the trunk. As the aspen leaves flutter, imagine they are chattering to each other. What might they be talking about? Do you see the aspen "eyes" (elongated branch scars on the trunk) looking at you?

Another way to experience this woodland is by stopping at creek crossings where children can feel the mosses that cover the rocks like green quilts. They may spy a water strider skating across the creek among floating aspen leaves. Four dime-sized shadows made by the water strider's legs dimpling the water surface are what children see first. Encourage them to slowly move close to the water-walking insect to see the tiny hairs on its legs. These help maintain its position and sense of movement on the water's surface. A pebble dropped into the stream sends the strider skittering to shore. However, when an insect falls to the water, its minute vibrations lure the strider to investigate.

Among the many wildflowers lacing this wooded canyon is the wild rose, so common it's hardly noticed by many hikers. But a careful look at a rose in flower or fruit may reveal an insect gall, an elongated swelling about the size of a cherry. Explain that a gall is formed when an insect lays its eggs on the plant. A child who takes a gall home and stores it indoors in a jar learns within a few days what lives inside one.

At 2.5 miles, the trail veers west, away from the creek, and begins its steep 0.5-mile ascent to the trail's end at Missionary Ridge. Those who prefer streamside explorations should turn around at this point.

Those continuing the 3-mile hike to Missionary Ridge get the best views from the top of a knob, about 200 yards northeast of where the First Fork Trail meets this "stock drive" trail.

No toilet or water facilities are available at the trailhead.

67. Potato Lake Trail

Location:	San Juan National Forest
Type:	Day hike or overnight camp
Difficulty:	Easy for children
Hikable:	May–October
Distance:	1 mile, one way
Starting elevation:	9360 feet
High point:	9800 feet
Maps:	San Juan National Forest, USGS Engineer Mountain

Driving Directions: From Durango, drive 28 miles north on US 550 and turn east on the signed Lime Creek Road. Continue 3.5 miles on this gravel road to a large lily pond on the right. The trailhead and parking area are just past this pond on the left. Access from Silverton requires driving 20 miles south on US 550.

The trail leading to Potato Lake (commonly called Spud Lake) is as friendly and fringed with interesting diversions as the sparkling destination itself—which can serve as a lunch site, a fishing spot, or an ideal overnight campsite. Recently graded and

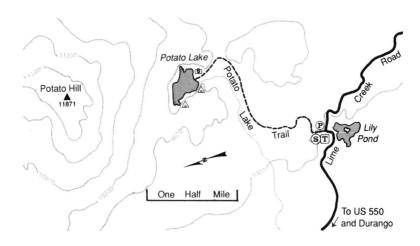

A family skips rocks at Potato Lake.

rerouted, this popular trail is now easy enough for beginning hikers.

Before setting foot on the trail, most children like to inspect the lily pond across from the trailhead. While they throw pebbles into the water (as children seem compelled to do at the sight of a pond), explain that the blanket of lily pads actually protects the fish and plants living under them from the heating effects of the high-altitude sun. The seeds of the lily's yellow flower were once gathered by Indians and ground into flour or roasted—with a flavor, some say, like popcorn.

A medley of aspen and spruce flanks both sides of the path that climbs gently for 0.25 mile to the new smooth, wide trail on the right. Potato Hill, also called Spud Mountain, peeks through the trees straight ahead. Engineer Mountain, a popularly photographed peak prominently visible from US 550, appears to the west of the trail followed by Graysill and Grizzly peaks.

Within 0.5 mile of this mountain display, the trail turns to the northwest where the amazing architecture of beavers awaits your inspection. In the recent past, only a few abandoned "lodges" remained in the pools on both sides of the trail. Now, prominent stick-and-mud structures bulge from the pond's still waters. Beavers store their food, aspen twigs and stems, in the lodge, which they enter via an underwater "door." Aspen tree gnawing keeps the beavers' teeth trim. Otherwise their choppers would grow so long they'd be useless and the animal would die of starvation! To feel the power these dam builders employ in their construction, children should touch the toothmarks gouged into aspen stumps littering the pond region.

Just beyond the beaver ponds, the lake opens to its full panorama. Potato Hill, a small 11,870-foot spud compared to its 13,000-foot neighbors to the east, the West Needle Mountains, is reflected in this spring-fed lake.

The trail can be followed in either direction around the lake, which offers a beach-like entry for wading on either side of the creek draining it. In early July, the lake's water temperature is barely warm enough for a refreshing dip. Young anglers will want to settle into the chair-sized rocks along the lake's shore for a relaxing afternoon teasing the trout-fed waters. On sunny days, gentle breezes stir up a sparkling, diamond-studded lake which, when pointed out to young children, adds a magical, imaginative flair to the visit.

A walk around the lake entails following the shore-side path and crossing a marshy area near the lake's northeast shore. Raspberries and strawberries growing along the shore are free to keen-eyed, nimble-fingered pickers.

The lake has several nearby level campsites and no camping permits are required.

68. Molas Trail

Location: San Juan National Forest
Type: Day hike or backpack
Difficulty: Moderate to challenging for children
Hikable: June–mid-September
Distance: 0.5 mile, one way, to overlook I; 1.5 miles, one way, to overlook II; 3.0 miles, one way, to D&SNGRR tracks
Starting elevation: 10,604 feet
High point: 10,160 feet at overlook; 8930 feet at railroad tracks
Maps: San Juan National Forest, USGS Snowden Peak

Driving Directions: From Silverton, drive 6 miles south on US 550, about 1.5 miles north of Molas Pass. Turn east at the sign for Molas Lake and Molas Trail, following the dirt road to the park-

Needles Mountains near Potato Lake

ing area. From Durango access to the trailhead is 43 miles north on US 550.

This is a delightful high-country ramble where sky-piercing mountains rim the horizon and wildflowers blanket the meadow. Hikers of any age can absorb this magnificence at two easily reached overlook points. Those who continue down into the valley meet the beautiful Animas River and have the option of returning to Durango or Silverton via the narrow gauge train. Backpack trips into the Weminuche Wilderness can start here.

Follow the road from the parking lot south to the Molas Trail on the right. The trail curves around Molas Lake veering southeast with the Needle Mountains looming straight ahead. Ask your companions why they think the mountains were given that name.

During the first 0.5 mile, as the trail winds around the willow bushes, watch for little birds darting in and out of them. White-crowned sparrows nest just beneath this greenery. Children who look carefully may discover the birds' hideaway. They may notice the air is warmer under the brush than above it, a temperature difference that allows more eggs to hatch.

In between the willow mats, look for herds of elephants— little red ones that is, flowering on stems standing 8 to 24 inches tall. Close examination shows the elephant's trunk, even its lower lip. Elk forage this wet meadow flower and its companion, the willow bush.

Families with very young hikers may want to walk just over 0.5 mile to where the trail reaches a small, rocky overlook of

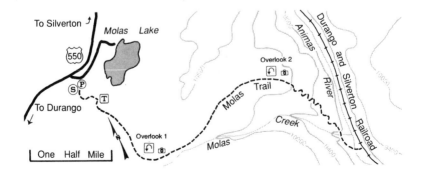

Walking the historic narrow-gauge tracks, Molas Trail

13,074-foot Mount Garfield, the western-most sentinel of the Grenadier Range. ("Grenadier" is another name for soldier.) Molas Creek, slicing through the shallow valley just below this perch, is on its way to the Animas River at the bottom of this valley. From here it's a fairly steep but short descent before the trail traverses an alpine wildflower garden for nearly 1 mile.

At 1.3 miles, the scene is one of a spruce-fir forest. After passing the sign on the left cautioning against cutting trail switchbacks, advise the hike leader that the path to the overlook point is on the right, near an aspen stand approximately 40 yards farther.

The rugged mountains of the Weminuche Wilderness fill the

views from the perch at the top of this spur trail. A thousand dizzy feet below them spills the Animas River. In mid-afternoon you have a good chance of seeing and hearing the Durango & Silverton Narrow Gauge Railroad on its return trip to Durango. The D&SNGRR is the longest continually operated steam train in the United States. The 1.5-mile hikers turn around at this point and follow the same trail back.

Those who continue the walk to the railroad tracks descend via switchbacks before crossing Molas Creek then meet the footbridge that spans the Animas River at 3 miles. Backpackers join the Elk Creek Trail on the other side of the train tracks at Elk Park, 0.5 mile south of here.

A delightful return route to Durango or Silverton is via the authentically refurbished coal-fired passenger train, which can be flagged at Elk Park. (Before leaving Durango or Silverton, meet with train officials to learn the proper technique for flagging a train.) Call 303-247-2733 for information on times and ticket prices.

Since the switchbacks are not steep, the return route on the same trail is a challenge most kids can meet—provided a fun, patient attitude is maintained.

69. Ice Lake Trail

Location:	San Juan National Forest
Type:	Dayhike or backpack
Difficulty:	Moderate to challenging for children
Hikable:	Mid-June–mid-September
Distance:	3.5 miles, one way
Starting elevation:	9850 feet
High point:	12,257 feet
Maps:	San Juan National Forest, USGS Ophir

Driving Directions: From Silverton, take US 550 for 2 miles northeast and turn left on a gravel road leading to the South Mineral Campground. Drive 4.1 miles to a parking area alongside the road just beyond the campsites. Ice Lake Trail begins on the steep hill on the north side of the road.

Ice Lake Trail is a deceptively challenging walk to a decidedly magnificent destination. Engineered with shallow switchbacks to prevent steepness, the trail leads to two Ice Lake basins, lower and upper. Both are rewarding destinations for eager dayhikers or overnight campers.

Gentle switchbacks through a softly padded forest floor begin the trail. At 0.3 mile, a spur trail to the right leads to a destination for little hikers: a waterfall splashing 400 feet down the granite wall. Hold on to little hands for this view. Return to the Ice Lake Trail.

The trail continues switchbacking for another 0.8 mile where a stout railroad tie serves as a footbridge across a clear creek. About 0.5 mile from here, the remnants of a mining structure stand nestled in aspens on the left side of the trail. Remind children that this and other patented mining claims should be treated with the same respect as private property.

The trail continues westerly through the blue spruce forest until it opens to the panorama of the lower basin at 2.5 miles. Though too shallow for fishing, Lower Ice Lake sits in a verdant basin offering splendid views of the mountains that rim this valley. The area surrounding the lake is flat, affording a multitude of camping or rest stops.

The trail to Upper Ice Lake remains relatively level until it reaches the rocky hillside at the end of the basin (3 miles). Bright

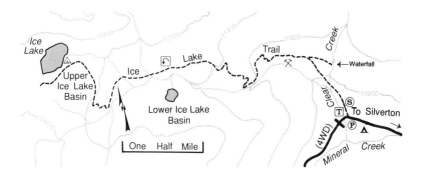

Lower Ice Lake Basin

columbine and Indian paintbrush canopy the trail as it climbs for a half mile.

During breath-catching stops, it's fun to watch and listen for noisy rock dwellers, the pika and the yellow-bellied marmot. More often heard than seen, the pika keeps busy all summer gathering his winter stash, which amounts to as much as five bushels! Look for his miniature bundles of grass drying on the rocks. In contrast is the marmot, lazily sunning himself while accumulating his winter food—nothing more than extra layers of fat! When snow blankets these mountains, the marmot's heart slows down to one beat every 12 to 15 seconds. (Have children compare that number to their own heart rates.) The pika, however, scampers about year-round, his furry claws helping him grip ice. Ask children which of the two mountain dwellers they'd like to be, and why.

While at Upper Ice Lake basin, help children identify each of the surrounding peaks. They are, from the south around west to the north: Fuller Peak (13,767 feet), Vermilion Peak (13,894 feet), Golden Horn (13,600 feet), Pilot Knob (13,738 feet), and U.S. Grant Peak (13,767 feet). Watch for an equally grand show at your feet. During mid- to late summer, herds of "little red elephants" show their rows of pink spikes to admirers who kneel close. "King's crown," with its fleshy leaves and maroon top hat, reigns over the wet soils.

Return is via the same path as the approach.

---

70. Jud Weibe Trail

Location: Telluride
Type: Dayhike
Difficulty: Moderate for children
Hikable: Mid-May–mid-October
Distance: 2.7 miles, loop
Starting elevation: 9000 feet
High point: 10,500 feet
Map: none

Driving Directions: From West Colorado Street in Telluride, turn north on Aspen Street, following it till it dead ends in a residential area. Limited parking is available alongside the street.

Telluride sits in a treasure chest of mountains jeweled by waterfalls and aspen glades. The best way to experience this alpine beauty is to walk the Jud Weibe Trail. Kids love seeing the ski area's steepest slopes from this trail and their parents appreciate starting a mountain walk right from town.

From Aspen Street, walk uphill to the metal footbridge spanning Coronet Creek. Before crossing the bridge, make a side trip to look at Coronet Falls, an 80-foot cascade reached by following the trail to the right for 0.25 mile. It's a delightful passage through stands of raspberries and wildflowers leading to a perfect destination for beginning hikers. Return to the bridge via the same path.

 From the bridge, the trail heads west, traversing somewhat steeply the south side of a red rock ridge. A 10-foot section along here is narrow; caution youngsters to watch their step.

Within 1 mile the trail turns east, leaving behind the oak and juniper of the dry slope and entering the greener pastures of an aspen forest. Between branches check out the views of the ski area and Bear Creek valley with a ripple of mountains beyond it.

The definitive viewpoint is from a clearing at 1.2 miles. From here, you can see Telluride as a tiny collection of miniature buildings nestled in a glacially carved valley. Bridal Veil and Ingrid Falls lace this scene dominated by 13,000-foot peaks. On calm mornings and late afternoons watch for large, brightly colored "birds" soaring above the peaks—they're hang gliders. Look for Lone Cone, a triangular-shaped peak standing alone on the southwest horizon.

If your hike occurs in mid-September or October, you'll notice distinct blocks of aspen splashing a uniform color across the slope. This uniform coloring happens because the trees share a common root system. After a fire has cleared a slope, aspens are the recovery trees, sprouting from their undamaged, underground feeding network. Look around, do you see any lone aspen trees?

By the way, trees do not really change colors. The greens, golds, and reds exist in the leaves all year hidden by chlorophyll,

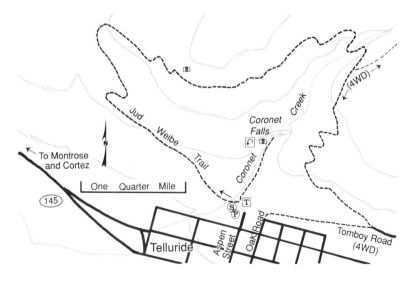

Crossing the bridge at Coronet Creek, Jud Weibe Trail

the tree's food producer, which is green. As autumn approaches, changes in the amount of daylight and temperature cause the chlorophyll to slow its production, which allows the tree's other colors to create a glorious show.

As the trail continues its eastern course, you will pass flower-dappled meadows and stands of aspens before it meets Coronet Creek at 1.8 miles. The smell of mint here can be traced to a tall, ragamuffin-shaped dusty-pink flower. Have children roll its stem between their fingers. They will discover it's square; a sure way to identify a mint if your nose is out of commission.

In its final descent, at 2 miles, the trail joins an old four-wheel-drive road flanked by bright yellow flowers with a name kids remember: butter-n-eggs. Turn left just past the trail sign posted on a tree then go through the gate. In 0.2 mile, the trail meets the Tomboy Road. Turn right and walk 0.2 mile to the top of Oak Street. Continue walking one block south to Galena Avenue, then turn right and walk one block west, returning to Aspen Street.

No toilet or water facilities are available at either trailhead.

71. Petroglyph Point Trail

Location:	Mesa Verde National Park
Type:	Dayhike
Difficulty:	Moderate for children
Hikable:	Mid-April–October
Distance:	2.8 miles, loop
Starting elevation:	6640 feet
High point:	6970 feet
Map:	Mesa Verde National Park brochure

Wheelchair accessible with assistance to Spruce Tree House only

Driving Directions: To reach the entrance to Mesa Verde National Park, drive 29 miles west of Durango or 10 miles east of Cortez on US 160. From the park entrance, pay an entrance fee and drive 20 miles to the museum parking area at Chapin Mesa. Hikers are asked to register at the sign-up stand at the Ranger Station adjacent to the museum.

On this loop trail, children discover how prehistoric Indians fulfilled their needs for food, shelter, and clothing while living in the high desert canyons of the Southwest. The trail circles a canyon and mesa top occupied by Anasazi Indians from around A.D.

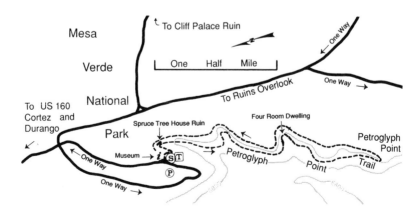

Petroglyph Point

600 until their abandonment early in the thirteenth century. The Petroglyph Point guidebook, available at the museum and Ranger Station, highlights the interesting plants and geology seen from the trail.

The trail begins at the museum on Chapin Mesa on the Spruce Tree House Trail. Descend 0.25 mile to an impressive Anasazi dwelling surrounded by tan sandstone cliffs and lush vegetation. Anasazi people started living here 1500 years ago. A spring trickling through the rock wall once supplied a community of some 100 people.

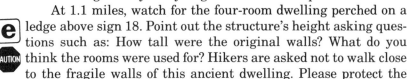

As the trail leaves this oasis, it meanders past stands of scrub oak, mountain mahogany, bitterbrush, serviceberry, yucca, and cactus. Explain that Anasazi people incorporated each of these seemingly fruitless plants into their daily lives. Encourage children to imagine ways they might use one of the plants.

At 1.1 miles, watch for the four-room dwelling perched on a ledge above sign 18. Point out the structure's height asking questions such as: How tall were the original walls? What do you think the rooms were used for? Hikers are asked not to walk close to the fragile walls of this ancient dwelling. Please protect the fragile nature of this unprotected prehistoric structure by staying on the trail.

Imaginations will be fueled at sign 19. Here children can feel ax grooves in a sandstone boulder where Anasazi people once sharpened their stone tools.

At mile 1.5, or sign 24, is the park's largest and best-known group of petroglyphs, which are images carved in rock. The Anasazi stood on a ledge or rope ladder here to chip a collage of designs through the darker layer of desert varnish and into the lighter sandstone beneath. Children may want to interpret the rock art.

This trail was made by park service personnel, not the Anasazi, who were adept at scrambling up slopes and leaping over boulders. When faced with a steep cliff wall, the "ancient ones" chipped notches into the sandstone, just deep enough to hold the front part of a hand or foot. Watch for this stone ladder in a small section of the trail just beyond the rock art.

From this point, the trail traverses the pinyon-juniper mesa top, circling around to the parking lot. Encourage kids to feel the spirit of "those who came before" as they quietly stalk this dry forest as the inhabitants once did.

In hot summer months, plan to explore this trail in the cool of morning. Although the park is open year-round, the trail is closed after snow falls. (Call 303-529-4461 or 303-529-4475 for further information.)

72. Dominguez–Escalante Trail

Location: Anasazi Heritage Center
Type: Dayhike
Difficulty: Easy for children
Hikable: Year-round
Distance: 0.5 mile, one way
Starting elevation: 7100 feet
High point: 7200 feet
Maps: none
Wheelchair accessible with assistance

Driving Directions: From Cortez, head north on CO-145 for 8 miles. Turn left on CO-184 and continue 1.5 miles to the turnoff for the Anasazi Heritage Center on the left.

This paved, wheelchair-accessible trail to an Anasazi ruin overlooking several mountain ranges will delight children of all ages. Interpretive signs along the way identify the local plants and explain how they were used by the Anasazi people about 1500 years ago.

All the plants you will see on this trail were important to the

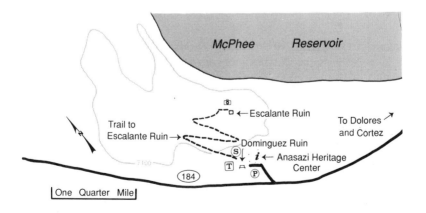

A family enjoying the high desert terrain

e people living here. Imaginative children might hear stone tools grinding corn, or children chasing a wild turkey through the brush. If they are especially quiet and watchful, they may see a horned lizard sunning itself.

For a preview of what lies ahead, stop at the Dominguez Ruin, located in front of the Anasazi Heritage Center. Have children point out the site's four rectangular rooms and the circular kiva. Examine the stone work here. You'll want to compare it to the masonry at the Escalante Ruin.

The trail to the Escalante Ruin begins at the picnic site just west of the Anasazi Heritage Center. This gently graded 0.5-mile trail ascends through stands of scrub oak, pinyon, and juniper.

The undergrowth, thick with yucca and cactus, will deter young turkey chasers from attempting to cut across the switchbacks.

The Escalante Ruin, named for the Franciscan priest who discovered this site in 1776, is at the top of the hill. The elevated viewing platform here offers a panoramic look at the area's peaks. Sleeping Ute Mountain, identified by its silhouette of a reclining Indian, is directly west. Help children find north by locating Lone Cone, once an active volcano millions of years ago and now a triangular peak located between two mountain ranges, the San Juans (northeast) and the Abajos (northwest). Mesa Verde is directly south. The lake below is McPhee Reservoir. Built in 1985, it flooded the largest collection of Anasazi sites known to archaeologists. Many of the artifacts collected from the site are housed at the Anasazi Heritage Center.

From the viewing stand, you can see the remains of the Anasazi village—a rectangular block of rooms, the larger ones used for living, the smaller for storage. Children questioning the petite size of the "living rooms" should be told that most Anasazi activities took place outdoors, sleeping being reserved for "indoors" on cold nights. Comfort was not an important factor. The walls forming a circular shape are called "kivas," underground ceremonial rooms. Ask children to point out the two kivas.

Observant youngsters may notice the masonry here is

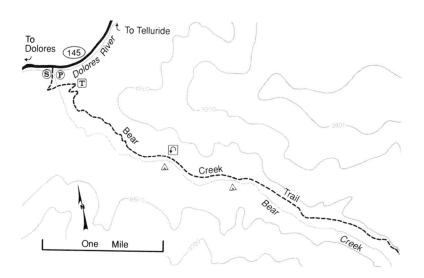

"fancy"; made up of rows of blocky stones alternated with bands of smaller stones called "spalls." This masonry style is one of the many signs indicating that the Anasazi who lived here traded with the Anasazi of the Chaco area (100 miles south) and tried to maintain a similar lifestyle. Ask children to compare the masonry of this ruin to that of the Dominguez site seen at the trail's start.

Be sure to reserve time to visit the museum at the Anasazi Heritage Center, open 9:00 A.M. to 5:00 P.M. during the summer, and 10:00 A.M. to 4:00 P.M. in winter. Operated by the Bureau of Land Management, the center houses more than two million artifacts, the product of the largest single archaeological contract awarded in the United States. Children will want to enter the center's rebuilt Pueblo I Pithouse or try their hands at grinding corn using a mano and metate—just as the Anasazi did more than a thousand years ago.

73. Bear Creek Trail

Location:	San Juan National Forest
Type:	Day hike or backpack
Difficulty:	Easy for children
Hikable:	June–October
Distance:	2 miles, one way, or farther
Starting elevation:	7900 feet
High point:	8200 feet
Maps:	San Juan National Forest, USGS Wallace Ranch

Driving Directions: From Dolores, drive 22 miles north on CO-145. (From Telluride, drive 44 miles south.) Watch for the green highway sign that reads "Bear Creek Trail" (1.7 miles south of the Priest Gulch Campground). Turn southeasterly into the dirt drive just beyond the sign. A wooden gate with a "no parking" sign blocks the drive for vehicle traffic. Park your car in the gravel clearing alongside the highway. Open the gate and walk 0.1 mile to the trail's beginning on the drive's north side. The

A tapestry of golden aspens and evergreens

trail passes behind private property before meeting the official trailhead 0.1 mile from the highway. Be sure gates are closed behind you.

The Bear Creek Trail winds through a forest medley of aspen, pine, oak, and spruce before it descends to a playful stream. Beginning rock skippers and expert anglers have fun teasing Bear Creek's pools and miniature falls. Campsites dot the flat, grassy area alongside the creek for another 2.5 miles.

For the start, Bear Creek Trail winds through a milky white stand of mature aspen trees as it gradually climbs almost 1 mile up and over a canyon rim. Fluttering in the slightest breeze, aspen leaves seem to whisper your passing. Stop to show children why the leaves "quake" so readily; its stalk is flat, attached at right angles to the leaf.

In less than 1 mile, the trail levels off and enters a wonderfully diverse forest complete with ponderosa pine, blue spruce, scrub oak, and aspen. The aroma of vanilla here comes from the ponderosa pine. Bearing 4- to 9-inch-long needles in bundles of three, this patriarch of the Southwest's south-facing slopes deserves a hug for its luscious smell. (Stay clear of its sap!)

The babbling sounds of Bear Creek increase as the trail descends the ridge slightly and meets it at 1.5 miles. The hike becomes a streamside meander for the next 0.5 mile as it edges a collection of pools and waterfalls that flow at a rate most kids can have fun with. Watching over this playful site are dark stands of spruce trees. To some hikers, the stringy black lichen that hangs from spruce branches gives the tree an eerie look. Little ones, however, like pretending the mossy growth is the forest gnomes' clothing hung out to dry. Black tree lichen was actually a common food, stewed with a bit of onion, eaten by various Indian people.

The pillowy-soft ground underneath these blue-green evergreens (often cultivated as Christmas trees) is comprised of old cone scales, the leftovers of many a squirrel's meal. However, the resourceful rodents use this collection as a midden or a storehouse for the berries, acorns, and pinecone seeds they collect each fall. Children enjoy searching the midden for the squirrels' entry hole.

At 2 miles, the trail enters an open meadow with several camping sites edging it along the creek. Here, too, are a number of perfect pockets to lie back in and get a squirrel's eye view of a world of wildflowers and grasses, capped by a Colorado blue sky. After your nap, head back on the same trail.

Another 4 miles upstream the trail enters alpine terrain and the headwaters of Bear Creek.

There are no toilet or water facilities at the Bear Creek trailhead.

74. Chimney Rock

Location: San Juan National Forest
Type: Dayhike
Difficulty: Easy for children to the lower ruins; moderate to the upper ruins
Hikable: March 1–September 30
Distance: 0.75 mile, loop, for guided tour
Starting elevation: 7200 feet
High point: 7600 feet
Map: Chimney Rock brochure
Wheelchair accessible around lower ruins only

Driving Directions: Chimney Rock entrance is reached via US 160, 45 miles east of Durango, or 17 miles west of Pagosa Springs. Turn south on CO-151, driving 3 miles to the Chimney Rock entrance gate and parking area on the right. All tours start from this locked gate.

During this guided walk, it's easy to imagine the era when Anasazi Indians occupied this high point, grinding corn in the shade of a juniper tree, performing secret rituals in a smoke-filled kiva, keeping watch over their land from the twin spires known as Chimney Rock.

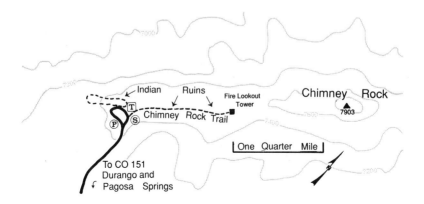

A kiva at the Anasazi ruin at Chimney Rock

The nimble-footed and those in wheelchairs are intrigued by unexplained remnants found at the area's two separate Anasazi dwelling sites, and children delight in using the "fire-finder" at the lookout tower near the upper ruins.

The San Juan National Forest Service conducts daily tours from May 15 to September 15, starting at 9:00 A.M. (an additional 11:00 A.M. tour is given four days a week during July and August). Groups in vehicles meet the guide for the 2.0-hour trip at the gate beside CO-151 then drive another 2.5 miles to the upper parking lot.

The tour starts west of the parking lot following the paved trail around a cluster of Anasazi sites considered "Mesa Verde" in style. Point out the large, rectangular rocks forming the walls. Each dwelling here was occupied by a single family, with the great kiva being a community center (women were allowed in only on special occasions). Archaeologists studying this site are stumped by the purpose of the two rectangular bins in the great kiva. Encourage children to imagine their use 1000 years ago.

Another puzzling prehistoric feature is the foot-wide circular basin etched in a rock slab near the end of the paved trail.

This wheelchair-accessible loop portion of the trail ends back at the parking lot. The tour to the upper ruins continues from here stopping within 0.1 mile at the set of three circular dwellings. When Anasazi women married they often built their homes next to their parents' dwellings. What might be the story behind the three structures here?

As the trail climbs nearly 400 feet to the upper ruins, the highest known Anasazi site, point out the Piedra River Valley to the west, farmed by an estimated 2000 Indians. Share with children the special feeling of knowing they are walking the same path the Anasazi used daily carrying jugs of water from the river to their homes. At your feet, look for fossils in the rock that hint of the inland sea that covered this region millions of years ago.

The dwellings and kivas situated near the two Chimney Rock pinnacles are "Chaco" in construction style. Notice the walls made of small rock layers alternated with large ones. These two-story (at one time three-story) homes were like apartments, housing several families. The two kivas are considered "clan kivas," used only by certain clans. Discuss with children the similarities and differences of the upper and lower sites.

In the fire tower adjacent to the sites, the panorama map helps to identify the rugged peaks of the San Juan Mountains. Those who focus their sights (binoculars needed) on Companion Rock, the wider pinnacle next to Chimney Rock, may see the peregrine falcons that summer there. Their nest is merely a depression in the rock. Because this bird of prey migrates to Mexico, where use of the pesticide DDT is extensive, its eggs break easily. Listed as an endangered species, the peregrine falcon population is increasing due to federal and state laws protecting it.

To sign up for the tour, call the Pagosa Ranger District at 303-264-2268; a donation is requested. Water and food are not available at Chimney Rock. Toilet facilities are located at the upper parking lot.

75. Lobo Overlook and Continental Divide Trail

Location: Rio Grande National Forest
Type: Dayhike or backpack
Difficulty: Moderate for children
Hikable: Mid-June–mid-September
Distance: 0.5 mile, one way, or farther
Starting elevation: 11,700 feet
High point: 12,000 feet
Maps: Rio Grande National Forest,
USGS Wolf Creek Pass

Driving Directions: Wolf Creek Pass is located on US 160, 36 miles west of Del Norte and 28 miles east of Pagosa Springs. The road to the overlook is just east of the divide on the north side of the highway. Drive 2.5 miles up this steep, two-wheel-drive road to the radio tower where the parking area for Lobo Overlook is located. The road is accessible to passenger cars after the snow is cleared in early summer.

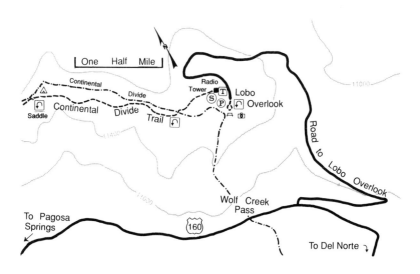

The southern San Juan Mountains from Lobo Overlook

This easily accessible trail along the spine of the Rocky Mountains is open to most anyone destined for the southwest corner of the state. Little ones may walk as far as the Lobo Overlook where lines of peaks and ridges fill the skyscape like an ocean of rough waters. Their bigger brothers and sisters following the trail to the west are lured by meadows bursting with showy wildflowers.

From the radio tower parking lot, the 0.3-mile walk south to the Lobo Overlook whets the visual appetite. The sea of mountains here means more to very young lookers when Wolf Creek Ski Area and the thin stripe of US 160 are pointed out. (Guardrails edge this cliff top viewpoint, but eager little hikers may need special watching.) As you stand facing north, explain that a drop of rain falling on your left shoulder is destined for the Gulf of Mexico. Those drops falling on your right will end up where?

The hike begins in the stand of spruce trees on the west side of the radio tower. The trail's first 0.5 mile is easy to follow as it crosses the ridgetop winding through an alpine meadow and enters a cluster of spruce and fir trees. In this coniferous gathering, your companions may notice a tar-like substance coating the ends of the lowest spruce branches; it's called black snow mold. Spruce trees can reproduce when snowpack holds a branch against the ground through the spring months. But if the snow lingers too long, snow mold takes hold, which can eventually kill the tree. Look for spruce seedlings started from mature branches. The 0.5-mile destination is at the start of a large meadow just past the spruce-fir forest.

Within the first mile, the trail dips down to the south avoiding a steep ridge climb. It then enters a flower-painted alpine bowl. Across this valley, point to Treasure Mountain. Its tresses of timber have been clearcut in a more natural fashion as opposed to the square blocks usually used in clearcutting. What is the purpose of clearcutting? (Almost always logging. Occasionally fire prevention and habitat improvement warrant it.) Does this clearcut look natural?

While peering across these mountainscapes, chances are good you'll ⊃py a small group of elk grazing. The high-altitude food (grasses and shrubs) they're stocking up on contains as much as 40 percent more nutritional value than that found at lower elevations. This is because plants of this terrain are generally small, so their food value is concentrated. What other reasons might cause animals to live at high altitudes during the summer? (Besides cooler temperatures and fewer people, fewer insects are the driving force. In addition to biting elks' faces and eyes, the flying pests lay eggs on the animals' skins.)

After climbing back to the ridgetop at 1.6 miles and then descending into a long valley, the trail meets a saddle, or low point, along the Continental Divide. Numerous campsites and lovely views make this 2-mile walk an ideal destination for dayhikers and backpackers. Unlimited opportunities for longer treks exist on this trail. The return hike from this point is via the same trail.

No toilet or water facilities are available at the trailhead. Picnic grounds adjoin the Lobo Overlook.

Appendix
Wheelchair-Accessible Trails

The following is a selection of Colorado's wheelchair-accessible trails. Since trail conditions are an important factor for wheelchair users, it's best to call the number provided before planning a trip.

Name	Park/ Nearest City	Length/Surface	Phone
High Line Canal Trail	Denver	see Hike 1	(303) 575-2757
Crown Hill Park Nature Preserve Trail	Denver	see Hike 2	(303) 278-5925
Niedrach Nature Trail	Denver	see Hike 3	(303) 659-6005
Enchanted Mesa–McClintock Nature Trail	Boulder	see Hike 10	(303) 494-0436
Central Garden Zone Trail	Colorado Springs	see Hike 14	(719) 685-9045
B.P.W. Nature Trail **	Colorado Springs	see Hike 17	(719) 636-1602
Williams Fork Boardwalk	Dillon	see Hike 28	(303) 830-9004
E. Alfred Marquard Nature Area	Buena Vista	see Hike 32	(719) 395-8797
Maroon Lake	Aspen	see Hike 36	(303) 925-3445
Hallam Lake Loop	Aspen	see Hike 37	(303) 925-5756
The Grottos	Aspen	see Hike 38	(303) 925-3445
Roaring Fork Braille Trail **	Aspen	see Hike 39	(303) 925-3445
Poudre River Trail	Fort Collins	see Hike 43	(303) 221-6640
Bear Lake	Rocky Mountain NP	see Hike 49	(303) 586-4459
Sprague Lake Nature Trail	Rocky Mountain NP	see Hike 50	(303) 586-4459
Never Summer Ranch	Rocky Mountain NP	see Hike 53	(303) 627-3471
Fish Creek Falls	Steamboat Springs	see Hike 56	(303) 879-1722
Animas Overlook Trail	Durango	see Hike 65	(303) 385-1283
Spruce Tree House	Mesa Verde NP	see Hike 71	(303) 529-4475
Dominguez–Escalante Trail	Cortez	see Hike 72	(303) 882-4811
Chimney Rock	Pagosa Springs	see Hike 74	(303) 264-2268
Rock Canyon Trail	Pueblo	4 miles/paved	(719) 561-9320

**Designed for the sight impaired

Name	Park/ Nearest City	Length/Surface	Phone
Colorado River Trail	Grand Junction	3 miles/paved	(303) 244-1642
Pueblo River Trail	Pueblo	20.5 miles/paved	(719) 545-9114
Yeoman Park Trail	Eagle	0.23 mile/composite material	(303) 328-6388
W. O. Roberts Nature Trail	Boulder	0.4 mile/smooth crushed rock	(303) 830-7792
Summit Lake Trail	Arapaho NF	0.24 mile/smooth crushed rock	(303) 830-7792
Doudy Draw	Boulder	0.5 mile/paved	(303) 494-2194
South Mesa Trail*	Boulder	0.25 mile/crusher fines	(303) 494-2194
South Boulder Creek	Boulder	3.0 miles/gravel	(303) 441-3440
Centennial Trail	Boulder	0.8 mile/paved	(303) 441-3440
Teller Farm	Boulder	0.25 mile/gravel	(303) 441-3440
Mount Sanitas Valley	Boulder	1.2 miles/gravel	(303) 441-3440
Wonderland Lake	Boulder	1.43 miles/paved, gravel	(303) 441-3440
Cottonwood Trail	Boulder	1.2 miles/paved, gravel	(303) 441-3440
Wilderness on Wheels	Grant	0.8 mile/boardwalk	(303) 988-2212
Platte River Greenway	Denver	11.5 miles/paved	(303) 698-4900
Washington Park	Denver	2 miles/paved	(303) 698-4900
Stapleton Park Trail**	Denver	1.25 miles/natural	(303) 964-2500
Highway 7 Trail	Estes Park	2 miles/paved	(303) 586-5331
Spring Creek Trail	Fort Collins	5 miles/paved	(303) 221-6660
Waneka Lake Trail	Lafayette	1.2 miles/cinder	(303) 665-5588
Rio Grande Trail	Aspen	2 miles/paved	(303) 920-5120
Dillon–Keystone Trail	Dillon	3.5 miles/paved	(303) 453-2561
Memorial Park Trail	Colorado Springs	1.2 miles/paved	(719) 578-6640
Horseshoe Park	Aurora	1.5 miles/paved	(303) 695-7160
Utah Park	Aurora	1.5 miles/paved	(303) 695-7160
Meadowood Park	Aurora	1.1 miles/paved	(303) 695-7160
Expo Park	Aurora	1.7 miles/paved	(303) 695-7160
Arkansas River Trail	Pueblo	9.5 miles/paved	(719) 543-6006
Fountain Creek Trail	Pueblo	4 miles/paved	(719) 543-6006
Pueblo Reservoir Trails	Pueblo	16.5 miles/paved	(719) 561-9320
Yampa River Trail	Steamboat Springs	4.1 miles/paved, gravel	(303) 879-2060

* Available summer 1992   ** Designed for sight impaired

Index

MAUREEN KEILTY has been a special needs teacher, summer camp program director, and most recently, a free-lance writer. She is the author of several books (including *Camping and Trail Guide to Southwest Colorado's Natural History*) and many articles. She lives and writes in Durango, Colorado.

Durango, Colorado resident Dan Peha has been a professional photographer for more than 15 years. His images have appeared in many magazines, including *National Geographic Traveler*, *Travel-Holiday*, *Ski*, and *Bicycling*, and have been used in a number of books and calendars. He has studied with Ansel Adams.

THE MOUNTAINEERS, founded in 1906, is a non-profit outdoor activity and conservation club, whose mission is "to explore, study, preserve and enjoy the natural beauty of the outdoors... " Based in Seattle, Washington, the club is now the third largest such organization in the United States, with 12,000 members and four branches throughout Washington State.

The Mountaineers sponsors both classes and year-round outdoor activities in the Pacific Northwest, which include hiking, mountain climbing, ski-touring, snowshoeing, bicycling, camping, kayaking and canoeing, nature study, sailing, and adventure travel. The club's conservation division supports environmental causes through educational activities, sponsoring legislation, and presenting informational programs. All club activities are led by skilled, experienced volunteers, who are dedicated to promoting safe and responsible enjoyment and preservation of the outdoors.

The Mountaineers Books, an active, non-profit publishing program of the club, produces guidebooks, instructional texts, historical works, natural history guides, and works on environmental conservation. All books produced by The Mountaineers are aimed at fulfilling the club's mission.

If you would like to participate in these organized outdoor activities or the club's programs, consider a membership in The Mountaineers. For information and an application, write or call The Mountaineers, Club Headquarters, 300 Third Avenue West, Seattle, Washington 98119; (206) 284-6310.

Call or send for catalog of more than 200 outdoor books published by:
The Mountaineers
1011 S.W. Klickitat Way, Suite 107
Seattle WA 98134
1-800-553-4453